I0570889

PRAISE FOR
A PILGRIM'S GUIDE:

"If you've ever been curious about walking the Camino, this sacred book brings you straight to the center of that deeply spiritual experience. Renee Baribeau blends introspection with practical advice, making the gifts of that extraordinary journey available to spiritual seekers everywhere."

KATHERINE WOODWARD THOMAS,
AUTHOR OF THE NATIONAL BESTSELLER
CALLING IN "THE ONE"

"Where I see a path, Renee Baribeau sees a journey. With a unique eye for the desires of the soul, her insights and perspective are always a breath of fresh air. *A Pilgrim's Guide to Walking Wisdom* will take you on your own inner pilgrimage through symbol, synchronicity, and surrender to the hope and wisdom that are never far from those with eyes to see."

DR. PAULA STONE WILLIAMS, TED SPEAKER,
AUTHOR OF *AS A WOMAN*

"*A Pilgrim's Guide* is the perfect accompaniment to any journey of the soul—whether you are traveling to a foreign country, walking the Camino, or are an armchair traveler. Renee's wisdom and insights, and those of the people she met along the path, will help guide you on the mindset, intentions, rituals, and questions that can make your own journey one of transformation. If you are in a time of transition, looking for meaning, on the healing path, or feeling a vague calling, this book can be a wonderful spiritual companion." LISA TENER, AUTHOR OF *BREATHE. WRITE. BREATHE.*

"Renee Baribeau has written an amazing book where she leads us through her pilgrimage on the Camino de Santiago. Never an easy pilgrimage for anyone, Renee did it in the true way of making a choice to keep walking through the physical challenges while going into a deep place of introspection. Going past mental beliefs and diving deeply into universal teachings—this is where true magic comes from. *A Pilgrim's Guide to Walking Wisdom* is a beautiful book for our times, filled with practical guidance for personal growth and healing."

SANDRA INGERMAN, WORLD-RENOWNED SHAMANIC TEACHER AND AWARD-WINNING AUTHOR OF THIRTEEN BOOKS, INCLUDING *SOUL RETRIEVAL*

"Like a mash-up of the timeless spiritual wisdom of *The Four Agreements* with the practical guidance of *The 7 Habits of Highly Successful People,* this book offers an eleven-ingredient recipe for living a meaningful life served on a platter of page-turning adventure."

LORI LOTHIAN, ASTROLOGER AND AWAKENED DREAMER

"Anyone who has been on a pilgrimage can relate to the dilemmas and insights Renee Baribeau shares from her Camino journey. Those who haven't should read this book before embarking on their own. This concise companion guide offers wisdom for almost any spiritual journey, whether a weekend camping retreat or a longer pilgrimage to a sacred site. Baribeau distills archetypal encounters into universal truths, making them accessible to pilgrims of all faiths—or none. Through down-to-earth, relatable tales, she reveals the divine essence of truths discovered along the path."

SUZANNE A. FAGEOL, M.DIV, M.S.D., EPISCOPAL PRIEST, SPIRITUAL GUIDE, AND COUNSELOR

ALSO BY
RENEE BARIBEAU:

Winds of Spirit: Ancient Wisdom Tools for Navigating Relationships, Health, and the Divine

Wind Walker's Wisdom Oracle (card deck)

A PILGRIM'S GUIDE TO WALKING WISDOM

....

11:11 Insights

RENEE BARIBEAU

Enlightenment Productions

SEATTLE, WASHINGTON

Grateful acknowledgement is made for permission to reprint an excerpt from "The Journey" from DREAM WORK *by Mary Oliver. The copyright credits for this work may be found on page 173.*

Copyright © 2024 by Renee Baribeau. All rights reserved. No part of this publication may be reproduced, distributed, or transmitted in any form or by any means, including photocopying, recording, or other electronic or mechanical methods, without the prior written permission of the publisher, except in the case of brief quotations embodied in critical reviews and certain other noncommercial uses permitted by copyright law. For permission requests, contact the author at the website below.

Enlightenment Productions / Renee Baribeau
Website: ThePracticalShaman.com

Cover design by Ryan Dwyer and Renee Baribeau
Editing and book production by Stephanie Gunning
Illustrations by Iulian Thomas

A Pilgrim's Guide to Walking Wisdom / Renee Baribeau
— 1st edition

Library of Congress Control Number: 2024921087

ISBN 979-8-9913973-0-8 (paperback)
ISBN 979-8-9913973-1-5 (ebook)

To pilgrims everywhere.

*To Don Deffendorf, who inspired this
book before taking his final pilgrimage
across the rainbow bridge.*

CONTENTS

A PILGRIM'S GUIDE

PROLOGUE

" Solvitur ambulando. "

LATIN FOR "IT IS SOLVED BY WALKING"

This book contains eleven insights drawn from the over one hundred-mile walk I undertook with friends in spring 2024 on the *Camino de Santiago,* a historic pilgrimage route ending in Galicia, Spain. Preparing for the Camino wasn't just about packing the right gear—it was about preparing my heart and mind. This journey invited me to release expectations and to walk with trust, knowing that what lay ahead would unfold as needed. These insights have been gestating in my soul for over three decades, inspired by past pilgrimages to sacred places, including a trek on horseback in Chile, a Native American vision quest, a thirty-day solo art sojourn, and two hiking trips to the sacred mountains in Peru.

Before leaving home, my life was packed full, like the oval-shaped cans of sardines and anchovies I would soon be introduced to at the Mercado do Bolhão in Porto, Portugal, which are artfully decorated with colorful illustrations. The colorful rows of sardines mirrored the tight organization of my commitment: every task and responsibility neatly confined to the boundaries of routine.

It was around that time I received an email from my old friend Victoria who said she was planning a trip to Portugal and Spain. For over two decades, the call to walk the Camino de Santiago had whispered in my ear, showing up after moments of loss, depression, or during retreats in nature. It was a persistent reminder that there was something more to discover—something new to invite in, an urge to break free. What finally got me to put on my walking shoes was her saying yes to my suggestion that we co-lead a group of pilgrims on that trip. In issuing the invitation to share an adventure, I was finally answering a call that had become urgent.

Changes were swirling all around me that felt like a windstorm, unsettling everything I thought was stable. Despite my professional success as an author and property owner, and being nourished by my career, I felt old and edging toward irrelevance. To me, the pilgrim's path appeared to be an opportunity not just to reset, but to transform.

The first time I saw the yellow arrow, I knew I was on the right path. These arrows, along with the clamshell markers, became silent guides, offering comfort. They reminded me that even though the way ahead was uncertain, I just needed to trust that I'd see the next marker when I was ready. Much like in life, we miss the signs when we're distracted, but when we pay attention, the way is always revealed.

I wasn't alone in needing and wanting to make a shift. On the trail, I met many fellow pilgrims whose reasons for walking mirrored mine. One day, I walked with a woman who had spent years in a high-powered corporate job. She had a steady career, financial success, and what some would call an "ideal life," but her soul felt disconnected. "I need to find my way back to my work as a healer," she told me. The Camino was her space to listen, to walk, and to rediscover the wholeness she felt she had lost.

Another pilgrim explained, "I'm between homes and hope the Camino will help me figure out where to live next." Like me, she had reached a crossroads, and each step was bringing her closer to achieving clarity. "I don't have the answers yet, but walking is helping me hold space for the questions."

After building a small business from the ground up, one fellow traveler was ready to say goodbye to the version of herself that ran it. "It's time," she said, "to sell my business, close this chapter of my life, and walk into the unknown."

Yet another pilgrim, a restaurateur from France, was walking to make peace with a recent project that hadn't gone as planned. She carried disappointment like a heavy stone in her chest, but each day on the Camino lightened that burden. "We walk to let go," she reflected, "and to make space for new dreams."

As I walked, I couldn't help but notice the *apachetas,* piles of stones left by pilgrims. Each stone represented something: a burden, a prayer, a memory. I, too, carried stones, both literal and metaphorical, and it wasn't until I reached these sacred markers that I felt ready to release them. Just like the woman from France who carried disappointment in her chest, I realized that the stones in my pocket weren't just physical—they held the weight of expectations, fears, and rigid structures that I no longer needed.

On one of my solo walks, I came across an especially large cairn at a crossroads. I paused, reached into my bag, and pulled out a stone I'd been carrying since the beginning. I held it in my hand for a moment, letting the weight of it sink in before blowing into it with my breath, then placing it on the pile. As I walked away, I felt a lightness, a freedom. The Camino, like life, invites us to leave behind what no longer serves us, so we can move forward with grace.

For me, the journey was about releasing the pressure of a structured life. And because life has a mirroring aspect to it, I often found myself walking alongside people who were living their own versions of structure, some more rigid than others. One woman was a traveler at heart, someone who loved experiencing new countries and tasting their cuisine. "This," she said as we walked past a cafe, "is the beauty of life—exploring, seeing, tasting, being in it all." The Camino was her way of staying connected to the world. The joy she radiated reminded me that every pilgrim's reason to walk is different.

Why was I walking? Back at home, the winds of mortality had been stirring. A close friend had passed away. This loss was followed by a young man's tragic death a few months later. I had barely recovered from the shock of it when another death—that of the tenant who'd been renting my desert home—threw me into a fresh spiral of grief and logistical nightmares. What was supposed to be a peaceful return to my winter sanctuary had turned into weeks of forensic investigations and biohazard cleanups. It felt like the fragile suspension bridge of my life was shaking beneath me, threatening to collapse.

Following this cluster of unhappy events, I diagnosed myself with PTSD, from which it would take many kinds of spiritual counseling, EFT, and medicine work to heal. Even as I was healing, the series of my losses continued, culminating with the death of a longtime acquaintance, a carpenter whom I had hired to finish some work on my home. To shield myself emotionally, I threw myself into my business activities, but it wasn't until I started preparing to walk the Camino as a pilgrim that I felt the winds of healing begin to shift in my direction.

In Greek mythology, Theseus, a prince from Athens, seeks to end the suffering of his people by confronting the Minotaur, a monster born from the infidelity of Pasiphaë, wife of King Minos of Crete. The Minotaur, half-man and half-bull, is a symbol of shame for the king. He has imprisoned it in a complex labyrinth. Ariadne, the king's daughter, has fallen in love with Theseus, so she gives him a ball of thread to guide him through the maze. This thread allows him to navigate the twists and turns, defeat the Minotaur, and retrace his steps to safety.

Like Theseus, I needed a thread to navigate the labyrinth of grief and overwork I found myself trapped in. What helped me begin to find my way through was windwalking on a mountain near the home of a friend I was staying with while my death-desecrated house was being renovated. Each step I took became an act of healing, an opportunity to process the deep anger and pain I was carrying. Ultimately, the Camino would bring me resolution.

In addition, I found my thread in the people I met as I walked the Camino. Through our shared stories, it became clear that the Camino is never just a physical journey—it is an invitation to release what no longer serves us and move toward a deeper understanding of ourselves. Each of the women on our trip was following her heart, whether to heal from grief, rediscover joy, or simply move forward, step by step. I had let my life become so crowded with obligations that I'd forgotten how to move at my own pace. Walking the Camino was my chance to find my way back to center, back to myself.

Coinciding with this period of personal healing and restoration, I noticed a strange phenomenon occurring. Everywhere I looked, I kept seeing the number eleven. This had started a few weeks before my tenant's death when I was preparing for the winter solstice celebration I lead each year for my online community. For that celebration, I keep a sacred bonfire burning in my yard for several days while other spiritual seekers light candles on their altars. The purpose is to combine our energy, set intentions, and invite blessings for the new year.

The synchronicity of seeing elevens in many different contexts assured me that I was on the right path, guided by forces greater than myself. I have long known that, according to numerologists, the number one signifies a new spiritual beginning. An eleven is like a one, except with double the intensity. And the number 111 is even more intense than that. In those days, whenever I happened to glance randomly at a clock, it always seemed to be reading 11:11 or 1:11. I took this synchronicity as a message to pay close attention to whatever was going on.

Throughout history, the people of many cultures have believed in the significance of omens and divine providence. In ancient Rome, fortune-tellers interpreted the will of the gods by studying the flight patterns of birds. And due to two typhoons that blew up suddenly and the Mongol fleet in the thirteenth century, protecting Japan from invasion, the medieval Japanese believed in a *kamikaze* ("divine wind"). These examples illustrate how nature will guide and protect us.

I, too, have encountered signs. The synchronicity of seeing so many elevens seemed like one of them.

I hoped a new beginning would be coming for me in Spain. Although I had gotten complacent in my life, I was now fantasizing about a time in the future when I would venture out to be "me" again— whatever that meant. No understatement, my future plans were murky. Until I received the email from my friend, my dreams were vague and diluted. Due to the confirmation of the elevens, I immediately recognized this trip to Spain as an opportunity for the initiation of a new, grand dream for my life.

Just as seeing the same number everywhere we go can be an omen, nature can show us signs, or correspondences, that are meaningful. As I walked the Camino de Santiago, I met a man who was overworked and burned out from years of doing too much, like me. When he shared his story, it reminded me of a blackbird that once appeared on the inside ledge of my kitchen window. This was a correspondence.

Beyond the curiosity of how the blackbird could get into the house, for me there was the deeper question of why the bird was there and what message it carried. Weeks later, both my father and stepfather departed suddenly. Dad had a massive stroke the day after the grand opening of my farm-to-table bistro. Fred, my mother's husband, died instantly of a massive coronary while finishing a run.

That blackbird was the first and last ever to enter my home unbidden. Because its visit took place before I had any significant spiritual training, I did not know what to make of it.

When the man I was walking with told me, "I was looking for a way out, but now I realize I need a way back in," and I thought of the bird, I knew to pay close attention. He had come seeking a sense of balance, and with every step, he was finding it.

Interpretation of signs and correspondences is an art because different signs will mean different things to each of us. A feather lying on the ground may go unnoticed by those for whom it has no relevance, and yet seem meaningful to me when it catches my attention. And while a feather for me may indicate that I am heading in the right direction, for you it may be a sign to turn around.

There are so many places calling for our glance. I believe a walking pilgrimage can slow our roll enough that we begin to consciously pay attention to the lichen on a tree, which may be looking back at us with its tree eyes. Learning to accurately read signs on the road as a pilgrim and in natural settings takes patience, trial and error, and discernment.

Even seemingly devastating experiences can be experienced as interventions from grace if you learn to look at them humbly, from the perspective of a pilgrim seeking wisdom. Pilgrimage offers every wanderer a means to prepare internally to face and overcome great challenges that lie ahead and hope for a new beginning after they come and go.

As we learn in elementary school math class, the number one is magical because any number multiplied by it remains the same. Seeing 11:11 everywhere I went was the starting point of my pilgrimage. Like a guiding star, it was pointing the way forward for me. Even before I received the announcement of the upcoming pilgrimage through Portugal and Spain, 11:11 was relentlessly pursuing me, like messages about an Amazon Prime Day sale. The digital clock in my car would flash 11:11; a 1, 11, or 111 would be my gate number at the airport; after a purchase, the receipt would read $11.11; and texts and emails from friends were time stamped at 11:11. This happened consistently for six months before, during, and after the trip.

Following the walk, I continued to be stalked by ones and elevens—so many, in fact, that I felt like I had to ask myself, *Am I looking for them or do they appear to me spontaneously?* On Facebook, I saw a post from the official group of the Camino showing a meme about the number of walkers arriving each day to Compostela by various routes. I scrolled the records back to June 10, the day our group arrived there after walking for eleven days and saw an eleven right in the middle of a two and a six in the statistic of 2,116 pilgrims who arrived that day. I then flew home on July 11. Amid the weary Facebook algorithm that selectively shows users ads and posts, I saw a friend post that a package she received had arrived at 11:11 AM that morning.

The purpose of this book is to share a few guiding principles I learned from walking the Camino and encourage you to embark on your own pilgrimage to answer the deeper longings of your soul. Our walks can be short or long and their level of effort easy or hard. Yet there's something about walking that always connects us to the earth and our souls in a way that teaches us what matters.

When I walked the Camino, I walked with the intention to heal my troubled spirit. Toward this end, I made a habit of asking a question at the beginning of the day and tried to be receptive to the form in which the answer came to me, without prejudging it. According to one pilgrim I met along the journey, a person who has walked many sacred paths through Europe, "The Camino is a day-by-day, hour-by-hour adventure. Always make appropriate adjustments in the moment."

The Camino offers every pilgrim a way to walk through their story, releasing what no longer serves them and inviting in the new. Whether they are releasing a home, a relationship, or a career and closing a chapter in life or needing to reconnect with life, the journey teaches us that our dilemmas may be solved by walking.

Solvitur ambulando.

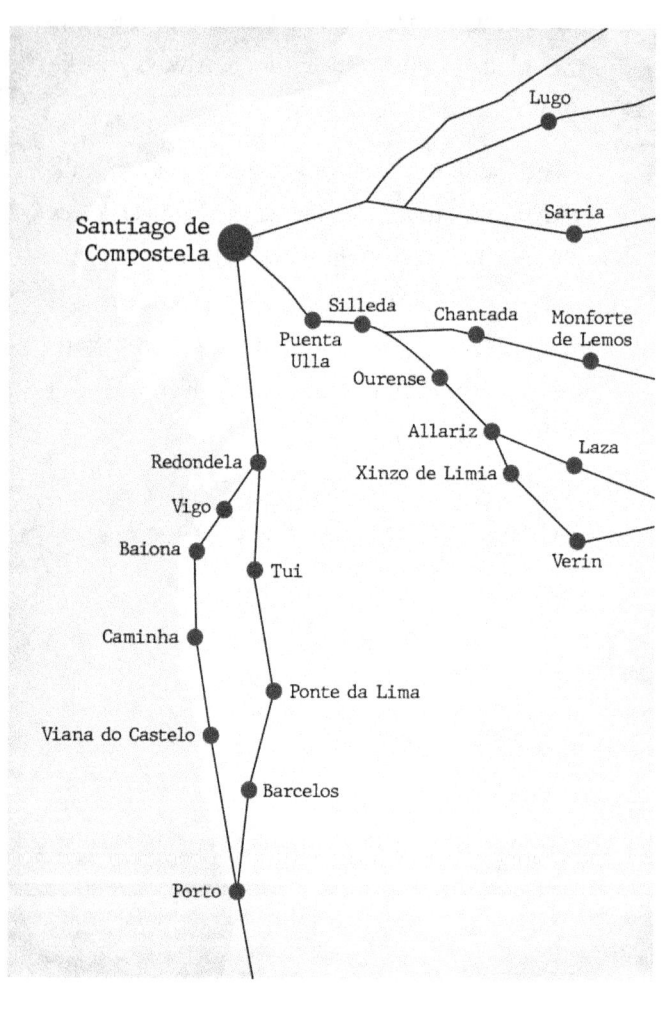

Lugo

Sarria

Santiago de
Compostela

Silleda

Chantada

Monforte
de Lemos

Puenta
Ulla

Ourense

Allariz

Laza

Xinzo de Limia

Redondela

Vigo

Baiona

Tui

Verin

Caminha

Ponte da Lima

Viana do Castelo

Barcelos

Porto

....

Make a Sacrifice

"I know that I hung on a windy tree
nine long nights,
wounded with a spear, dedicated to Odin,
myself to myself,
on that tree of which no man knows
from where its roots run."

"THE HÁVAMÁL"

Pilgrimages always involve some level of sacrifice. Sometimes, it's a deliberate offering of comfort, like the man I read about in one of the many Facebook groups dedicated to the Camino who chose to walk barefoot. His feet were calloused, battered, and bruised. He wanted to feel every rock, every grain of dirt beneath his feet, surrendering the luxury of shoes to stay grounded in each moment.

"It's my way of staying connected to my recovery," he shared. In every painful step, he found peace.

When Odin, the One-Eyed All-Father, sacrificed himself by hanging from the World Tree, *Yggdrasil,* for nine days and nights, he sought wisdom and knowledge of the runes. His self-sacrifice for greater wisdom and enlightenment embodied the transformative journey of a pilgrim. Whether a pilgrimage—a quest for insights—involves hanging yourself upside down from a tree, traveling across continents and oceans to embark on a walk to a sacred site, or stepping away from your daily routines for the purpose of meditation or reflection, it will always involve a sacrifice.

In the twenty-first century, while most contemporary people no longer sacrifice livestock to appeal to their gods, seeking to curry favor, in many traditions making a periodic sacrifice continues to be a spiritual practice. A pilgrimage qualifies.

Becoming a pilgrim demands that we set aside the mundane. It requires stepping out of our routines and making a genuine request for guidance. And it involves taking the often uncomfortable initiative to press pause on doing things we love to do and the familiar so we may open our minds and hearts to seek signs and embrace synchronicities.

MAKE A SACRIFICE

Some sacrifices are monumental and impact millions. Writer J.K. Rowling faced countless rejections before becoming a literary sensation with the Harry Potter book series. She pushed forward as a struggling single mother on welfare, sacrificing financial stability in pursuit of her dream. Similarly, athlete Michael Jordan made the heart-wrenching decision to leave the NBA at the height of his basketball career to pursue a short-lived stint in baseball, knowing he was leaving behind what he had mastered.

Our decisions, whether monumental or small, shape the lives we lead and impact those around us. Making a clear-eyed decision often requires us to evaluate our values, priorities, and long-term aspirations. Sacrificing the comforts of routine in pursuit of clarity—like a pilgrim on a journey—can open us up to deeper insights. For some, it might be seeing repeating numbers, like 11:11, as I did, signaling alignment with divine support.

For you, a decision worthy of reflection might be as personal as where to school your children, what kind of cancer treatment to pursue, or whether to downsize your home so you may prioritize travel in retirement. These choices, big or small, invite us to walk with intention, guided by the wisdom of both heart and head.

Frequently, the sacrifices we may need to make are a part of a decision. We are deciding either/or, or choosing between multiple options that preclude one another. Our values, our relationships, and our finances may compete as determining factors.

Sacrifice, I've learned, isn't always about giving up material things. It also can be about shedding identities that no longer serve us. A woman in our group with whom I walked one day had been running her own yoga studio until recently, only to realize that her success left her feeling empty. She told me that she sold it all, not knowing what would come next.

"The Camino is my space to let go and find something new," she confided in me as we trekked together. It was a risk to follow this path, a sacrifice of her security in pursuit of the unknown, but she felt the call to make a change, just as I did.

I was at a crossroads in my life, in my sixties and debating the best moment to begin taking my well-earned social security pension, knowing this monthly stipend would allow me to restructure how I was spending my days. During the previous decade, I had worked double time. While holding down a very full corporate job, I wrote and published a book, built a house, gathered a tribe of likeminded individuals online, and started a weekly podcast. The pandemic mainly disrupted my leisure activities. COVID came, and while others were excited to stay tethered to their homes, I was sad because a trip I had planned to Germany for Easter 2021 to see a traditional version of the Passion Play was canceled. Giving up on the trip was my sacrifice. In exchange, my online teaching skyrocketed.

For decades, I have strived to create balance within the tapestry of my life. But when my workload doubled, the sacred balance I'd nurtured for so long was thrown askew.

Once the public health restrictions related to the pandemic were lifted, I experienced the activities I'd been missing, such as the joyful obligations of family, including three weddings (two requiring cross-country airplane travel) and a memorial service to commemorate the death of my older sister. These were highly significant events I would not have missed for the world.

But in addition, Facebook had reconnected me to high school friends who were retiring *en masse.* I could see how they were enjoying an easier lifestyle of travel and leisure than mine. A resentment began brewing in me about the financial necessity of continuing to work a full-time job while I was also building a sustainable teaching practice.

My life was out of balance. Though I'd always defined myself by how hard I worked, the fast pace of my corporate job no longer satisfied me; instead, it felt grueling. It was time for me to transition from being just a "hard worker" to being a true leader.

I wasn't alone in having this type of realization. One day on the Camino, I met a man who had spent decades climbing the corporate ladder, relentlessly chasing the next promotion. He eventually realized that, despite his success, he wasn't happy, so he made the bold choice to quit his job, sell his belongings, and embark on a pilgrimage to discover what truly mattered to him. The security and status he had known were replaced by the unknown path ahead.

The man walked across multiple continents, one step at a time, in search of balance and simplicity. Along the way, he met his current life companion. His story is a reminder that when we release a dream we've clung to, we often make room for something better to unfold.

After three months of preparation, I became a pilgrim when I left home to have an adventure on the Camino. Walking five hours a day, often in shaded eucalyptus forests, gives you plenty of time to think. As I reflected on life, I shot dozens of short videos and hundreds of pictures on my phone to capture and, later, share memories of the experience.

Originally, I planned on writing by hand in my journal every day, but this did not happen. I started out that way on day one, but then, on day two, the water bladder I was carrying to hydrate myself while hiking malfunctioned. Everything inside my backpack got wet, including the seventy-page, wide-ruled spiral notebook I brought with me from home with the intention of filling it with musings. Two water-diffused cntrics and a manifcsting cxcrcisc got wet and stuck together as they dried.

My journal writing did not make it past the second day of this hiking regimen. I sacrificed it. It was enough to get up, brew a cup of coffee, put all my scattered clothes back into my "cheater" bag (an overlarge duffel bag on wheels that could be carted from town to town by the courier whom our group leader had hired for this purpose), and bring it downstairs by eight o'clock each morning before the group left the hotel on foot.

In hindsight, the early morning baggage call required another sacrifice from me. At home, I generally wake up at will, make my coffee, then go back into my bedroom to write or leisurely assemble the elements of my day while sitting in my bed with PJs on. Alarms have never been my friends, although I will set an alarm if I have an important rendezvous or a plane to catch. Most days, I rise long before 7 AM, especially when I am writing in response to a nudge from Spirit. Typically, I will spend two hours alone before facing off with the day.

On the trek to Santiago de Compostela, my body was thrown off its normal schedule. While my friends and I had chosen to walk the coastal Portuguese route that takes the pilgrim 118 miles at sea level, instead of the 500-mile route from France that traverses complicated mountain slopes at high altitude, it was a daily endurance test. In addition to the eight-hour time difference between Spain and Washington State (where I reside much of the year), I was forced to adapt to a new bedroom setting daily. Reliable sleep and my daily routine were surrendered.

Thinking about this experience reminds me of a recent episode of my podcast, *The Shaman's Cave*, when my cohost, Sandra Ingerman, mentioned that early in her healing career, her spirit guides told her that people seeking her assistance would need to make a sacrifice in exchange for the healing she was offering. Better results were granted by Spirit when people traveled for the session or skipped a cup of coffee at Starbucks to pay for a class or service.

The age of information has its benefits and its setbacks. When I was mastering the healing arts, I needed to go in person to meet my teacher each week. This meant driving thirty minutes each way, and spending many hours with her. Our sessions included spiritual preparation, building a fire from kindling and logs I would gather, assembling a lodge, waiting for the fire to be welcoming of the volcanic stones we wanted to heat in it, and then waiting some more. Once our Inipi ceremony was complete, before the community would gather for food, we would break down the lodge and neatly fold and stack the blankets we had used. No one could eat until a Spirit plate holding an assembly of potluck offerings was placed outside to thank nature for the food. The same group met weekly for many years.

One morning during my pilgrimage to Compostela, I made my daily video post at 11:11 AM while standing in front of a forest. In it, I spoke about suffering versus sacrifice. It received many comments on social media. A Sundancer friend made a good point about being careful with the word *versus*, as it creates a mindset of opposition and conflict. We live in an age where oppositional forces are air-bound and move swiftly from place to place.

I dare not add that energy strand to this story. For me, walking the Camino was a personal sacrifice of my morning routine and comfort, an offering of physical exertion made in exchange for the benevolence of the Wind Spirits with whom I work. My request was for help to organize the next cycle of my life in alignment with my highest authority.

My vision of sacrifice lines up with a translation posted on Facebook by a fellow shaman who was a former nun. The root meaning of the English word *sacrifice* derives from the Latin *sacrificium.* More specifically, from *sacer/sacra/sacrum,* an adjective meaning "set apart from the secular or profane for the use of supernatural powers," and from *facere,* a verb meaning "to make."

One could argue that I am a privileged White woman who could afford to pay for a "bougie" version of the Camino trip. Instead of chancing the availability of a bed and risking a poor night's sleep by staying at the public *albergues* (hostels) that are the cheapest accommodation option on the trek, I stayed in three- and four-star hotels.

Hard work and good luck have afforded me luxuries that many other pilgrims do not have. I had two pairs of good shoes—Merrill ankle boots and Hoka walking sneakers—in my full suitcase. Along the trail, I ate whatever I wanted whenever I wanted it. I could easily stop for snacks and cappuccinos. As you already know, there was a luggage service that moved my large duffel bag from town to town so that I could carry just my small backpack and adjustable walking sticks with ease.

After reading through the comments on my video, I found myself reflecting on the nature of sacrifice. Would a mother's sacrifice—perhaps of going without new shoes so her children could be provided for—be greater than mine? Sacrifices often arise from love, but there always comes a moment when we must choose to walk for ourselves.

I walked for a day on the Camino with a woman who shared that after decades of putting her family first, she finally chose to put herself first on the journey. "I've spent my life caring for my children and my family," she said. "Now it's time for me to give something back to myself." For her, the Camino wasn't just a pilgrimage of the body, but a deeply personal gift to her soul. She was walking a path toward rediscovery and renewal.

Sacrifices, in the end, are personal choices, shaped by our unique lives and callings. In her life, the mother had made one kind of choice, and I had made another. My service in life has been to Spirit, and to fostering community and connection rather than to raising children. Every path has its own rewards and tradeoffs. I've been a spiritual pilgrim for most of my life, from attending Girl Scout camp, even when others had moved on, to hiking mountain peaks in the United States, Peru, and Chile—all in pursuit of knowledge and wisdom. Every journey had included my own form of sacrifice and reward.

This new journey cost me over a month of wages, required the use of all my saved-up vacation time, and caused wear and tear on my body that would take time to balance afterward. It was a strenuous journey. Many back home watched from the "sidelines," thanking me for my service of praying for them as I walked and sent them photo and video updates, knowing they would likely never take on this type of pilgrimage themselves. I could feel their support for me every day as I walked.

I never suffered once during the 118-mile trek. There were nights when my legs felt stretched beyond reconciliation. My feet hurt from carrying the weight of my body, and there were blisters on my heels. A few massages helped, as did the occasional hotel bath. Still, with each new dawn, or at least in the morning, by the 8 AM breakfast I was ready to embark on the next leg of the journey and march on.

There was always the energy of the other pilgrims that I would encounter along the rocky trail. One moment I could be alone in the forest struggling to find my determination to continue, then I'd come upon others struggling to keep walking too. It was the combined energy of me, them, my travel companions, and all the pilgrims who came before us, as well as nature, that kept me moving forward.

The spirits must have been happy with me and my efforts because I felt rewarded. Simple things, like toilets, would appear when I had to go. Cafes were well placed along my route, too. A ham and cheese baguette near midday was the perfect accompaniment to hiking. It would nourish me at 11 AM when I was ready to eat my late breakfast. Passersby greeting us with a *"Buen Camino"* also provided me with the impetus I needed to carry on.

As the final miles of the day unfolded, the presence of fellow pilgrims walking at a brisker pace became a lifeline. Catching a tailwind from their pace provided energy and flow. Their steady rhythm and the cheerful clacking of their shoes provided a harmonious backdrop, inspiring me to push forward when my own steps began to wane. The sound of a group approaching from behind was more than just a welcome; it was a walker's song that infused me with renewed energy and a sense of belonging.

Reflecting on the journey, I realized how the sacrifices of time, money, energy, and comfort transformed into personal triumphs on the Camino. Each step gracefully carried me from one day to the next, reminding me of the numerous treks I had undertaken throughout my awakening journey. From leaving my home and beloved cat behind to seeking solace in the embrace of nature, every pilgrimage demanded its own toll. Whether enduring frosty nights in a tent on a high-altitude peak or traversing Patagonia by horse, each experience reinforced my resilience and deepened my connection to the natural world.

These sacrifices were not merely challenges to overcome but essential components of my growth. Nature remained a steadfast source of solace and wisdom, offering answers that only the wilderness could provide. As I walked the Camino, the cumulative weight of past sacrifices lifted, replaced by a profound sense of purpose and fulfillment. The Camino was more than a physical journey; it was a testament to the endurance of the human spirit and the transformative power of shared experiences.

In the quiet moments of reflection and the camaraderie of fellow pilgrims, I realized that each sacrifice made was a stepping stone toward a greater understanding of myself and the world around me. My journey toward balance wasn't made in isolation.

As one day on the Camino gracefully moved into the next, I carried with me the lessons of perseverance, community, and the unwavering belief that every sacrifice was paving the way for a richer, more meaningful life.

The Camino teaches us that sacrifice is not always about giving something up, but about opening ourselves to what might come next. Often, when we let go of what we thought we needed, life presents us with something greater than we've ever imagined possible.

Reflection Questions

Throughout the book, at the end of every chapter, I will invite you to reflect on the meaning of the chapter and how it might apply to your own life, beginning here with the topic of *sacrifice*. Whether you decide to walk to receive an answer to a question, sit with the question for a few minutes, or write about it in your journal is up to you. Your pilgrimage will be of your design.

Let's begin with these questions.

Have you ever given up something significant in your life and then received a spiritual gift or insight?

What does the concept of *sacrifice* mean to you, and how has it shaped your journey?

In what ways can you honor the sacrifices you've made and acknowledge the paths that they've led you down?

How might you make intentional sacrifices now to align more closely with your highest purpose?

What is one specific sacrifice you are unwilling to make to further your personal growth or spiritual journey?

 I've prepared reflection worksheets that you can take on your walks with you. To download them, use the QR code that you see here or visit: bookwalkersclub.com.

....

Say Yes to the Call

"Let everything happen to you: beauty and terror.
Just keep going. No feeling is final."

RAINER MARIA RILKE

Saying yes to the call of pilgrimage requires a leap of faith and an act of courage. As an adventurer heading to an out-of-the-way place, you may get lost, step out of your comfort zone, and even duel with your inner demons, like fear.

One morning, I headed north on my own early from the Albergaria Quim Barreiro, our last seaside hotel on the Portuguese section of the Camino. Even alone, I felt a growing connection to the group. The prior afternoon the group had spent a fun-filled afternoon poolside, getting to know each other better, before gathering again for a group dinner. During this dinner, each participant pulled a Wind Spirit Card® from my carrying sack. I performed a ceremonial calling forth of their respective wind spirits to encourage them as they continued their adventure. The qualities listed on the cards—Strength, Trust, and Nourishment—would all be necessary for the long journey ahead.

It was clear from our conversations at dinner that people in our group were searching for their own personal Holy Grail, be it strength, optimism, or purpose. Much like the legendary quest of King Arthur's Knights of the Round Table, everyone was embarking on a journey not just across the land but within, seeking something deeply meaningful.

Spirit called the knight Perceval to undertake his profound spiritual quest for the Holy Grail. Like many of us on the Camino, his path was filled with surprising challenges for which he was often unprepared. Early on, Perceval was naïve. He initially came upon the Grail in a mysterious castle where, due to his inexperience, he failed to ask the one question that would unlock its meaning. In that moment, he missed an opportunity for physical and spiritual healing, prolonging his journey. He had to endure many more trials before he could return to the Grail and finally attain it.

Perceval's story reminds us that the answers we seek aren't always obvious; often they require deep internal reflection to uncover. I can relate. Much like Perceval, in my own journey, I, too, have found myself missing chances to ask essential questions and receive the healing that is available.

There have been moments when I thought I had everything figured out—my life, my purpose, and my spiritual path. After the catastrophe I experienced in my home over the holidays, it was clear that I did not. It wasn't until I set foot on the Camino that I finally began asking better questions.

And just as Perceval eventually returned to the Grail, wiser and more spiritually attuned, I had a realization after a long period of emotional wandering. But like him, I would endure trials before uncovering the deeper truth I was seeking.

By day three, the strain of walking for hours had begun to take its toll on my body. My feet ached, my legs felt heavy, and doubts about my stamina crept in. As I paused to adjust my boots, I noticed one of the women in our group wrapping her knee with quiet determination. She had injured it earlier, but rather than give in, she took a deep breath, secured the bandage, and carried on. Her resilience was contagious, a reminder that the journey isn't solely about the miles covered but about the courage to press forward despite discomfort.

That morning, it struck me how this woman's physical resilience mirrored the silent, internal struggles of another woman I met on the journey. Vanessa was a successful architect—wealthy, accomplished, and responsible for designing some of the most iconic buildings in her city. On the surface, it seemed like she had it all. She probably could have afforded a luxury vacation on a yacht, so what had drawn her to the Camino, a difficult endurance challenge? *Was she searching for something intangible?* The question lingered.

Spiritual journeys often require us to strip away the outer layers of our existence: to leave behind what society tells us should be enough so we can discover who we are without our stuff. Perhaps Vanessa wasn't walking to design something new but to find out what still felt missing. Success in the world of architecture might have satisfied her professional aspirations, but I sensed that, like the rest of us, she was searching for something deeper. Something that couldn't be drawn on a blueprint or constructed in concrete and steel.

As the days passed, I began to see that her presence wasn't that of someone who has her life totally figured out, but of someone quietly searching, while easily supporting others. Walking the Camino offered her space to explore a different kind of fulfillment—walking with people who unconditionally held space for her.

One evening at dinner, I noticed how Vanessa would listen quietly as others shared their stories, but she rarely spoke about her own. Her quiet presence reminded me that no matter how "complete" someone's outer life may seem to a beholder, we all carry unanswered questions and unmet needs within us. In a way, she mirrored a labyrinth—an intricately designed path leading to a center that requires time and space to traverse. Vanessa, like all of us, was searching for her center.

Vanessa reminded me that success in the external world doesn't always translate to peace within—although maybe it did for her. I never fully understood her reasons for walking the Camino, still her perseverance left a lasting impression. Sometimes, it's not about finding the answers but about embracing the questions along the journey.

That morning of the third day, after setting out early, walking solo, I met some other pilgrims from the United States while enjoying a coffee and my final *Pastel de nata,* a popular tart comprised of a thin layer of pastry and creamy custard. We made small talk, discussing the excellence of the local pastries. Although my favorite tart thus far had been one I ate fresh from the oven at a coffee shop near the Mercado do Bolhão in Porto after a steep uphill climb from the São Bento train station, this mid-morning tart was delicious. I said farewell to the folks from Washington State while still wiping crumbs from my lips.

I arrived at the water taxi landing early—at 10:11 AM, to be precise. Seeing as there were no other pilgrims to take across the river that would deliver me from Portugal to Spain, not even my touring companions, after waiting twenty minutes the boat captain loaded me into a sixteen-foot skiff and zipped me across the Miño River, then off-loaded me on a sandy beach and pointed for me to go left.

Victoria, our tour guide, had advised us that there were two possible trails we could take for the Camino upon arrival in Spain: We could either go right and take a short, steep walk over a hill or go left, like the boat captain suggested, and take a long, flat detour around the hill. She mentioned that former travelers told her the long walk around was not worth the added time.

Many times during the trip, I would discover that people had made up stories about the character of a particular day's walk. On this day, the travelers' characterization couldn't have been more wrong. Always follow your inner guidance, no matter what any guide or book says. I learned this lesson every single day as I walked across foreign landscapes.

Disembarking from the skiff, I felt an intuitive nudge to follow the long, flat detour around the hill. As I walked up the sandy beach toward the peaceful fishing town of A Guarda, I was greeted by a boardwalk that traced the coastline. It wound through a forest that felt almost magical. Near the start of the path, white footprints were painted on the boardwalk. When I stepped inside these prints and looked up, from my trajectory I saw a series of artworks spread across the faces of multiple trees. Each installation required several trees to complete a new scene. One of the most striking pieces was a white labyrinth, painted across three trees standing several meters apart.

After taking time to admire these artistic creations, I moved on, reflecting on the symbolism of the labyrinth as a journey in itself. At the last set of painted footprints, I met a fellow pilgrim—one of the few I encountered along this pristine stretch of rocky coastline. We marveled at the brilliance of the tree art, exchanging thoughts about its depth and beauty. She then shared her story with me: She had recently lost her husband. Because they had planned to walk the Camino together, after his passing, she decided to honor his memory by continuing the journey on her own.

Her pilgrimage, she hoped, would be a space for her to say yes to life again—a place and time to grieve, reflect, and ultimately find peace. Her sacrifice wasn't just in letting go of her partner but in embracing the destiny of an unknown future without him. With each step, she was discovering not only her own resilience but also the healing power of moving forward, no matter how painful.

The widow's story lingered with me as I walked alone for the rest of the day, contemplating the people I had loved and lost, and how they had shaped my own journey. The coastline stretched on, seemingly endlessly, and I felt both the weight and lightness of solitude. It wasn't until the distant buildings of the next seaside town came into view that I began to see other pilgrims wearing backpacks again.

Throughout history, seekers have been called to adventure. Some hear the call and say yes, and some hear it and say no. *Yes* takes us into the deep water of life. *No* keeps us in the shallows. Still, there is a deliberate moment in life when each of us must say yes to the summons of our spirits if we intend to experience a deeper, almost mythical, experience.

Your call to adventure may come when you least expect it. Mine came when I was stranded at the airport on Christmas Eve. I had just finished doing a fire vigil that lasted several days and ended on the winter solstice. I was tired but at peace. Then the phone rang. There had been a death in my rental house in Palm Desert, the town where I was headed for a month of rest and relaxation. I was shaken by the severity of the news and what it would require of me in response as a homeowner. Never had I ever had to cope with something so upsetting.

I realized in that moment, standing in the chaos of the airport, that this was no ordinary challenge.

The death in my rental house wasn't just a logistical crisis; it would become the catalyst that shook me out of my complacency. This death in my sanctuary forced me to engage in deeper inquiry: *What does* home *truly mean? Where is my spiritual home?* I realized I had been building my life solid on the outside, hollow on the inside. The call to the Camino wasn't just a call to undertake a demanding physical journey; it was also a call to undergo spiritual excavation. I had to tear down the old walls to find what was below them, at my foundation.

For some of us, the call to adventure comes in the form of a life-altering diagnosis. Adventures are not always pleasant. I remember how it was for a close friend after receiving the news of a cancer diagnosis. Her world turned upside down when she had to navigate the unfamiliar terrain of hospitals, treatment, and an uncertain future. Yet, in that chaos, she found a new path, one that led her to have a deeper connection with herself and her loved ones. Her journey became one of healing, not just physically, but also spiritually, as she said yes to the call to fight to live and to live fully.

Then there are those who experience unimaginable losses, like the death of a child, whose grief becomes a call to adventure. A couple I know faced this devastating reality, and their lives were irrevocably changed. Their call to transform their pain into something beautiful that honored their love was not one they would have chosen, but they embraced it, nonetheless. They turned their grief into a mission to help other bereaved parents, creating a community of support and understanding. Their journey through the depths of sorrow brought them to a place of profound empathy and resilience.

Natural disasters, too, can be catalysts for transformational adventures. When a hurricane destroyed a friend's home, he found himself standing in the rubble of what once was. His call came in the form of rebuilding not just his home, but also his life. He discovered a strength he'd never known he had and a sense of community as he and his neighbors came together to support each other. The storm, which initially seemed like an ending, became a beginning.

I have always believed that everything happens for a reason. I could have rationalized that the man who died in my home was free from pain. I also have always believed that every experience holds a lesson for us. *What was I supposed to learn from this?* Clearly, our karma, such as it was, had created an intersection between us.

Just as I got dumped on the beach near the long and winding trail around the hill and not at the simple trail that would have taken me up over the hill to the next hotel, I thought that day about how the artwork in the forest had served as a beacon of light for me on a soulful level. If I had taken the short route over the hill, I never would have seen it. Perhaps the care with which I renovated the property where the death occurred was the "route" I needed to take that holiday season.

Now, seven months later, I was hoping this long walk around the hill in Spain would reawaken my faith so that when I returned to Palm Springs, I could once again stay in the house where the death occurred without the memory of what happened constantly being triggered at night when I got up to use the bathroom and looked down the hall into the dark shadows. Neither EFT, counseling, shamanic journeys, conversations with friends, nor the therapeutic ketamine sessions I'd done had cleared the imprint of this experience from my mind entirely. Before the event, I believed the house would be my home again after the tenant moved out, my sanctuary—a place of safety and holy ground. But Spirit had a different plan for me.

Spirit was calling me home too, this time to go deeper into my journey as a pilgrim, someone who had said yes decades earlier to spending a lifetime as a healer. This trip to walk the Camino was my acknowledgment of my soul's purpose.

As I walked the long route around the hill that day, I reflected how, in recent years, I had become complacent with my spiritual awakening. Sure, I had present-moment awareness most days. But clearly that wasn't enough. After the "fiasco" in my home (which is what I had begun calling it), I began to look at how well organized I had been as I created my awakened life. After the death, I began to question everything about myself, my sense of security, and how I typically spent my time.

Under analysis, my life seemed like a perfectly decorated layer cake of safety. The bottom layer of cake was the security I got from home ownership. Then there was a mousse filling composed of two amazing seasonal locations, one a winter desertscape allowing me sun and warmth far away from the harsh gray winter weather of the Pacific Northwest, and the other a summer haven away from the scorching heat and dryness of the desert, a place to retreat among cool Douglas firs and hike while looking at spectacular views of the ocean. The top layer of cake was the financial security provided me by doing a job I liked, where I found meaning and a good use for my talents. The frosting atop this layer was decorated with peace-of-mind florets I gained through attending a weekly meditation group.

Unfortunately, the bottom layer was composed of stale cake. The death in my home that butchered my serenity like a ragged cut made with a serrated knife had revealed its presence. I saw that my awakening was really just a pleasant mindset created from years of saying positive affirmations and limiting myself from entertaining negative beliefs.

Basically, my life was a well-constructed specimen of delight until the day that I took a bite of the stale cake and knew it could no longer satisfy my sweet tooth.

It is easy to move through the cycles of experience when you are getting your way and the world is conspiring with you in your favor. But when the wind blows and the cake falls from the table and you find yourself sitting with a pile of stale crumbs, look around for the call to adventure.

My call to walk the Camino de Santiago came after a long dry spell of work, no play, being a responsible, loving family member, and enduring the COVID-19 pandemic. It took someone dying in one of my residences to realize that my true home was now where my paintings hung on Whidbey Island off the coast of Seattle, Washington. My sanity used to be wrapped up in my belief about what awakening was and how I could manage and control my frame of mind and experiences. But that illusion had shattered like a piece of cake flung on the floor at midnight by a hostile monkey.

If you are walking barefooted outdoors in darkness, you must walk carefully to avoid accidentally cutting your feet on sharp stones. That's how carefully I was walking through my life after the holidays. I was uncertain about my path until the email came from my friend Victoria with an invitation to come to Spain. This particular sender rarely reached out, so I was half expecting a different invitation. But as soon as I read the information about the trip, I replied, "I am in."

And so my journey began to walk the Camino. And I didn't fail to notice how our first phone call about the trip happened at 10 AM, with ones being my personal sign of being on the right path, guided by the universe toward my true purpose.

Reflection Questions

Have you ever felt called to step outside of your comfort zone? What was the result?

What inner questions or fears have held you back from saying yes to an important call in your life?

In what ways can you cultivate courage in the face of discomfort or uncertainty?

What are the external trappings in your life that may be distracting you from seeking deeper fulfillment?

How can you make space to say yes to a new adventure or challenge, even if it feels terrifying?

....

Preparation Is Key

*"It is not the map that should make sense of the land,
but the land that will make a map for us."*

TRISTAN GOOLEY

Preparation helps pilgrims assemble the mental, emotional, physical, and spiritual tools necess- ary for the transformational journey ahead of them. Beyond the physical act of packing, which we customarily do before we travel for work or go on vacation, making a pilgrimage requires us to explore the story living inside us. Specifically, we ask: *What is the wind propelling me to experience?*

When I was writing my book *Winds of Spirit,* each myth about a wind god or goddess I uncovered led to the next, helping me fulfill my purpose as an author. I followed the scattered pebbles of wisdom blown to me by the wind for years, as if assembling pieces of an ancient puzzle. In that process, the wind itself propelled me, helping me construct the puzzle of ancient knowledge, much like the wind propelled ancient sailing ships toward new shores.

This time my call to adventure came when I was mentally, emotionally, and physically drained. I hoped this pilgrimage would turbocharge my inner windmill, like a gust of wind reviving exhausted fan blades whose rotation has slowed over time.

As part of the preparation for our group's trip to Portugal and Spain, Victoria sent us a scallop shell necklace that had a red cross painted on it, along with the official pilgrim's passport—the *Credencial de Peregrino*—and our list of hotels organized by date. Busy with my packing, while I did mildly investigate these hotels to ease my mind that I would be comfortable, I did very little other reading about the trip. The history of the scallop shell remained a mystery until I arrived in Portugal.

The scallop shell, now the iconic marker of the Camino, has a rich lore. Some say it originated when the remains of Saint James were carried from

Jerusalem to Galicia, and a horse emerged from the sea, covered in shells. James was one of Christ's twelve principal apostles in the first century, and after the crucifixion he became a missionary spreading the word of Christianity as far as the Roman-occupied Iberian Peninsula.[1] Others say pilgrims carried shells to use as bowls.

Whatever the truth may be, the shell has become the symbol that marks the Camino, and everywhere you look, you will see scallop shells tied to pilgrims' backpacks. Contemporary pilgrims are like detectives in nature, looking for the next scallop shell sporting a yellow arrow pointing out the correct direction to go.

These yellow arrows, now so essential to modern pilgrims, have their roots in the vision of Don Elías Valiña Sampedro, the parish priest of O Cebreiro. He was a scholar of the Camino's history and a passionate advocate for its restoration in the twentieth century. Armed with a simple bucket of yellow paint, he began marking the way with arrows, ensuring future pilgrims would not lose their way. These humble markers have since become a lifeline for the countless souls who walk these paths, guiding them step by step through the twists and turns of the journey. Just as Don Elías studied and tended the historical paths with reverence, we too follow his arrows, knowing that every step is not just a movement forward, but into something greater.

For me, the symbolic yellow arrows and scallop shells marking the way were also pointing to something beyond the literal.

In hindsight, earlier pilgrimages I'd made to remote sacred sites, like the time I climbed Ausangate in Peru, a mountain measuring over 18,000 feet in elevation, taught me the value of preparation. Camping at high altitudes poses a unique challenge. Still, I was not as prepared as I could have been for the Camino.

While I thoroughly enjoyed walking as a present-moment experience, doing some advanced research on things beyond our hotel amenities would have enriched my journey. Exploring the terrain and learning about the local culture and historical significance of my surroundings would have made my pilgrimage even more meaningful.

If you ever walk the Camino de Santiago, I recommend that kind of preparation for you.

Of course, I wasn't a total slacker. When packing for the journey, I joined pilgrim Facebook groups, asked questions of friends who had walked before, and carefully read, and adhered to, the packing list. I knew that the survival skills I mastered at Girl Scout camp in my youth would serve me well too.

When planning for an adventure, preparation is key. Like Theseus, who relied upon the ball of thread given to him by the Cretan princess Ariadne to help him navigate the labyrinth successfully, wise pilgrims equip themselves with tools and a mindset that can help them overcome the turns and blind alleys they encounter on the trail. The internal maze of subjective perception is the ultimate obstacle.

Preparation requires incorporating activities that create a balance of mind, body, emotions, and spirit.

When I hiked the sacred mountains of Peru, where temperatures can rapidly fluctuate from 32 to 73 degrees Fahrenheit, my physical preparation took months. In the California desert, sporting goods stores do not stock winter hiking gear, so I had to mail order it. Compatible hiking boots needed to be broken in by walking on varying terrains over many miles. Taking trips up nearby mountains helped me with this. EBay became a good source of Gore-Tex clothing that would keep me dry and warm.

Once all my hiking gear was gathered and tested, it was important to find the right duffle bag to store everything I needed to carry with me, from a below-zero sleeping bag to tourist clothes for city adventures before and after the trek. The duffle and other necessities would be tied to a pack animal that would carry them for the hiking group as we struggled to persist on our feet at high altitude.

PREPARATION IS KEY

A prepared camper, I've found, is a popular one. In the mornings, using my Pocket Rocket portable flame and a coffee dripper, I was able to serve my companions hot coffee before breakfast. They loved me for it.

Physical preparation is only the first part of preparing for a journey. The pilgrim needs to prepare emotionally and spiritually, as well. Requesting guidance and clarity from the unseen realm can align you with answers to questions you have not thought to ask. It is sensible to spend time in meditation and prayer to strengthen your muscle of faith that everything under the sun is possible.

When I walked the Camino, I consulted spiritual mentors who'd previously walked the route to gather their insights on how to use the trip to grow as a person and to secure their blessings for my success. Engaging in rituals that centered and grounded me was essential, as this helped me connect deeply with my intentions for the pilgrimage.

Another word of spiritual advice: Pay attention to your dreams. And write them down because dreams can be slippery and fall through the cracks of your memory. Before, during, and after my trek, I dreamed of encountering a big brown bear. I did not remember the first dream until after the third dream that occurred a month following my return home.

The first night in Portugal, I dreamed I was sitting right next to a closed window, on a tall, wooden-backed chair. A cat was on a tin-topped enamel table next to me, which seemed to be inside a farmhouse kitchen. I looked up, and a black bear was right on the other side of a glass windowpane looking in at me. Even though it was night and dark outside, the bear's face was lit up—as were its immense paws and sharp claws.

Although frightened awake by the dream, I had noticed the glass between me and the bear, and I knew that the bear represented something deeper— a calling to be more present to the signs, and to pay attention. In my experience, whenever a bear shows up for me, there is always a period ahead in which I need to calm the chatter in my mind to deepen my experience.

A pilgrimage can be the starting point for a new experience, much like the bear that awakens and is reborn each spring after hibernation. Was my spirit bear awakening and calling forth a new vision for my life? I was intrigued by this imagery and felt certain that the insight from the waking bear would reveal itself in time.

Paying attention to your dreams before, during, and after a pilgrimage can provide you with vital information that your soul needs you to know.

After being jolted awake that first night from what was already a fitful sleep due to the time change between California and Portugal, I had to confront my prevailing fear about embarking on the Camino: that my physical abilities were insufficient to walk over a hundred miles in two weeks. The previous year, I had suffered an injury in my right heel.

I wasn't alone in my concerns about walking the whole distance. During a pre-trip organization call, several members of the group gave themselves permission to take cabs if needed. Hearing that "cabbing it" was allowable, as a playful gesture and group gift I had fourteen white hats embroidered with "El Cabino Babes" in shiny pink thread. My occasional roommate and trip cofacilitator, Loki, who was the de facto leader of the Cabino Babes, had a busy urban lifestyle and career that left her struggling to build her stamina through daily walks.

Perhaps the gift of the cap was also subconscious preparation for me. I'd struggle mentally the entire trip over the issue of taking a cab.

Truthfully, most members of the group didn't prepare extensively. Setting clear intentions for my journey—such as the intentions of finding peace and gaining deeper insights—helped me stay focused and emotionally resilient despite my anxiety. Later I recognized that mental preparation is an important aspect of endurance conditioning. Good mental conditioning, along with carefully chosen shoes, were both essential in giving my feet, legs, and mind the best chance of success.

Practicing mindfulness was a crucial part of my preparation. I took short *wind walks* on the bluffs overlooking Puget Sound—my name for a practice of walking to gain wisdom—where I focused on being fully aware of my surroundings, thoughts, and feelings. This helped me connect deeply with the purpose and intentions for the impending adventure, reinforcing my readiness for making a pilgrimage.

I arrived in Porto, Portugal, a couple of nights before our group's first meeting. My early arrival gave me a soft landing and a chance to acclimate to new time zone, eight hours different from my home.

Porto is perched on a hillside arising to the north of the Douro River. The balcony of my hotel faced south toward Gaia, where Port wines are made. As a nondrinker myself, this fact was more informative than useful knowledge; still, many in our group enjoyed some sips of rare Port along the trail.

It was an easy, flat walk along the ancient cobblestone path to get across one of the five bridges in the medieval harbor of Ribeira. On the first day, I took a boat tour of the harbor to see the evolution of the bridges and wrap my mind around where I was in time and space. Then I bought a ticket for the Hop-On Hop-Off bus, as I was feeling the side effects of travel, and did the full city loop for two and a half hours.

On the second day, I resumed my physical preparation by walking up the steep hill from my riverside hotel to the Mercado do Bolhão. Each step, despite being a challenge to move against gravity, reassured me of my ability to handle hills and cobblestoned streets. I covered approximately seven and a half miles, testing both my Hoka sneakers and my stamina. By the end, I felt physically, mentally, and emotionally ready for the trek. The next day I would change hotels to meet our walking group.

One thing I learned right away was that my iPhone was not going to be helpful for navigation; I got turned around and lost every time I tried to use its GPS as a map.

On our first night, the group gathered on the patio of Tapas N' Friends, a cozy café not far from our downtown hotel. Loki and I arrived slightly late, having gotten lost due to faulty phone navigation. Nevertheless, we brought the embroidered hats to gift everyone in the Wind and Stars El Camino group. Wine flowed freely.

After the family-style *tapas* were served—small, artistically designed dishes like codfish fritters and *batatas bravas* (crispy potatoes with a spicy aioli)— we led an icebreaker intuition exercise designed to bond the group. Each person received a slip of paper and a pen, writing down their initials before the folded papers were placed into the "El Cabino Babes" hat and randomly distributed. The task was to write an answer to the question, "Is there a message for me about this trip?" on the slip they received. We then took turns pulling out the answers and sharing these insights while trying to guess whose message we were holding.

The message delivered to me came from a striking European woman with long, blond hair who was sitting midway up the table from me. I was at the end. She had a commanding natural presence, exuding leadership without effort. Her note read: "Change is good, change is life. Don't stop changing. Everything from houses, destinations, people, habits, words, and beliefs will change."

After dinner, we treated ourselves to gelato and a stroll through the lively bistro neighborhood, and I called it an early night right after that.

In the morning, the group met and took a bus to our intended starting point in the small, charming seaside town of Viana do Castelo located on the northwest coast of Portugal. A town rich in history, Viana offered us a welcome place to begin our spiritual walk on the Camino de Santiago as we arrived on the thirtieth of May for the Feast of Corpus Christi. From the Basílica de Santa Luzia atop a prominent hill overlooking the Lima River Valley to the Gil Eannes Hospital Ship for cod fishermen located in the harbor, which is now a museum, the town boasted Old World charm and modern-day pride of a sort I had not felt in Porto. Members of our group bonded further over lunch by the harbor. The plan was to stay the night in Viana and set out the next day.

After spending time in the spa, I went for a late-afternoon stroll with some friends from our group and discovered a magical pathway of red roses, pink carnations, white lilies, bright orange marigolds, and big yellow sunflower petals laid throughout the main squares and small alleyways of the city. A procession was about to begin. My companions and I captured a front-row seat at a café to watch it.

Corpus Christi, a Latin term meaning "body of Christ," is a celebration of faith. It seemed like a perfect foundation for my own walk with Spirit. Experiencing this honoring tradition provided me and others in our group, regardless of our spiritual leanings, a solemn beginning to our mutual pilgrimage. It seemed as if the carpet of flowers and seeds had been laid out for us, and I felt the power of the prayer as we joined the procession with hundreds of other people, following the white-gloved priests carrying tall silver crosses and swinging thuribles of frankincense, moving steadily to the rhythm of the marching band toward the cathedral.

We were ready.

Reflection Questions

How do you prepare for significant events in your life? And is there more—or something else— you could do?

When have you ignored or dismissed a call to adventure because of a lack of preparation? How did this affect you?

What spiritual or emotional tools do you rely on to help guide you through challenges?

What have your dreams been telling you lately? How might they be preparing you for something that is to come?

INSIGHT FOUR

....

Take One Step at a Time

"Mend my life!"
each voice cried.

MARY OLIVER

Portugal and Spain invited me to mend my life. The tug to do so came ninety days before the trip began, at a point when I was exhausted from a long season of work and other life events. I mused, *How can this call be yanking on me when I've barely walked in months, prep time is limited, and my calendar is full until then?* My own bad advice to myself was, "You are going to be walking for many days, so you'd better rest up to save your reserves." I was behaving the opposite of an athlete in training.

The Camino de Santiago encompasses many routes throughout Europe that merge in Spain and end in Santiago de Compostela (Saint James of the Stars). It is one of three medieval pilgrimage routes dating back to the ninth century, along with the route to Rome and Jerusalem. A popular route, one used by roughly a third of pilgrims, is the Coastal Route, which is at sea level and follows the shoreline. It is considered one of the simplest ways to walk to Compostela, traversing both forests and beaches, and lodging in charming seaside hotels. Note, it was not easy for this pilgrim to walk 118 miles in eleven days, so I am grateful we took this spectacular route as it offered us refreshing swims in the Atlantic Ocean, great food, and amenities, including massages, along the way.

Our group of fourteen women began the journey on a trail heading north from Viana do Castelo. As we set out of the city that morning at 8:30 AM, after enjoying a lavish buffet, I called upon a guiding wind spirit to accompany us on our pilgrimage. In many spiritual traditions, wind is synonymous with Spirit, representing the breath of life and creation. Within my practice, the Wind Walker's Clan, we invoke various cardinal and regional wind gods and goddesses for their wisdom and guidance. To connect with a guiding spirit for our journey, I drew a card from a small deck I carry with me. On this day, the wind spirit that came forth was T̆haté, the Lakota Sioux messenger wind, who would offer us overarching guidance for the pilgrimage ahead.

For me, pulling T̆haté was significant, as I was planning on offering a daily gratitude prayer and sharing a two-minute message on social media at 11:11 AM every day of the trip, then walking for the rest of the day with a "how?" question in my heart.

A "how?" question is a way to frame an open-end experience. For example, my question one day was, "How can I have more spaciousness in my life?" After asking it, I walked on and watched for signs and synchronicities that could inform me of what would need to change to create spaciousness.

On a day when I was feeling left out from the group, I asked, "How can I create more group inclusion for myself?" Right after I asked, I rounded a corner to see a plot of land with a dozen sheep in it. I laughed out loud. There were no sheep in our group, but I did realize that to follow the lead sheep wearing the bell, I would need to be more flexible about my start time, and demonstrate willingness to walk as part of a group of pilgrims.

The first day out of Viana do Castelo, the path was sparsely labeled. As we reached the next town, there was a large farmers market underway, and it was there that the path split. Having options like this one would become a common theme of the journey. "Should I go right or left?" is an example of a closed-end question.

Some of our group headed toward the seaside path, while I and a few others opted to take a spiritual path up the mountain. I was gung-ho to make the journey count, so I headed up the hill following ancient stone walls covered in ivy. But my friends were faster than me and I soon found myself alone. Reaching the end of a lane, I immediately became lost and felt unsure of myself as there were no blue and yellow clamshell tile markers visible.

I witnessed how easily I can move into a state of disorganization when I feel uncertain of my next turn. Then I spotted a man, my first Camino "angel," who was pointing me in the right direction. He was a simple man, humbly dressed, who walked with me until I spotted the path. I sensed that this was his work: guiding wayward pilgrims such as myself to find their footing as they head out of town, so I gifted him a Euro before I pressed on.

The route I was on was not a busy trail. During this first day, I only saw a few other walkers, including two women from Ireland who spoke enough Spanish to converse with the Portuguese driver who stopped on the road to give us directions when we were all lost and unsure of which way to go. Portuguese and Spanish are similar tongues.

We were pointed toward a path that cut down into the woods, crossed a river, and had been one of the original paths of pilgrims. The trail through the woods, used by locals and pilgrims who've lost the main route, felt magical as it wove down by a farm, an abandoned chapel, and an ancient watermill. Hydro power systems in Portugal are known as *azenhas do mar* ("watermills of the sea"). These traditional watermills are ingeniously designed to harness the energy of flowing water for various practical purposes, but primarily for milling grain.

The presence of water channels along this path meant I could stop and run water over my hands and face, a ritual which connected me more deeply to the land and the experience and washed away my fatigue.

Another notable aspect of this journey was how I kept crossing paths with the same women throughout the Camino. While thousands of people walked the same trail, there were many I never saw or spoke with. Yet, one woman from that dinner appeared several times along the way, including at the final destination of the Cathedral. Though we exchanged nothing more than warm smiles and nods, there was an unspoken camaraderie in each meeting—an acknowledgment of shared persever-ance: "You got this" or "Here we are again at the end of another day."

Many years ago, I was hiking in Peru. Though I had not prepared well enough to scale the Andes Mountains to their highest double-digit elevations, I was strong-willed and determined. Pride played a major role in my decision to attempt the summit. Despite my lack of real mountain climbing experience and living at sea level, I wanted to show off to a woman I was trying desperately to impress that I could keep up with her and do it. Part of the adventure, before making camp on the 14,500-foot-high mountain that was our ultimate goal, involved doing smaller daylong hikes. One was a walk up the salt flats in Maras. The other was a visit to Machu Picchu.

This was my first visit to the sacred site of Machu Picchu. I clearly remember inching up the stone path, one small step at a time, to the top. There was a vista point about halfway up, where I rested. As I looked out over the sacred monument, I thought, "This is good enough for today. It is an amazing view from here." Then the wind spoke, "Renee, enlightenment is not found halfway up the mountain." That insight pushed me to continue.

I heard that same guiding voice during the twelve- to fifteen-mile daily walks on the Camino— over uneven ground, stones, hills, seaside boardwalks, and winding city streets. Seeing my physical discomfort, Loki persistently encouraged me to come with the Cabinos, the subgroup of three (or sometimes four) people who were using taxis to shorten their treks, turning their pilgrimage into more of a restful holiday.

As I wrestled with my expectations—*Am I walking the "right" way or should I be more relaxed?* —

the Camino mirrored my inner battle back to me. Loki, with her infectious laugh, would tempt me to take the easy route: a cab. Each time she did, it was as if the universe was gently inquiring, through her, "Are you walking to prove something or to discover something?" Then, as I reconsidered Loki's playful offer, I would ask myself, *Am I walking to endure suffering or walking out of spiritual curiosity?*

Each night, I would allow myself the possibility of traveling the easy way. This lasted until the next morning, when my legs eagerly carried me forward into the new day's adventure. My body knew the answer was "No thank you."

"Keep walking," it said.

Most days were a push, walking between five and seven hours. Sometimes I walked alone, guided by white butterflies flitting along the path.

On the second full day of walking, we were heading toward Estrada Baiona A Guarda. The sun was rising toward its zenith, casting a golden glow over the landscape. The hillside sloped gently to one side, while the expanse of a field opened to the ocean on the other. I tuned in to the natural symphony around me—the chirping of birds, the distant crash of waves, and the rhythmic crunch of gravel underfoot. My steps felt sure and light that day. A strong rhythm carrying me forward.

Up ahead, I spotted the youngest woman from our group, her pace noticeably slower, her focus inward. Earbuds in, she was walking steadily but clearly feeling the strain. I caught up with her just as the tinny sound of music leaked from her headset.

"Mind if I join you?" I asked, offering a smile. She looked up, surprised, pulling out one earbud. "Not at all," she replied, though her eyes showed signs of fatigue.

"I've been enjoying the natural soundtrack today," I said, gesturing to the birds and ocean. She smiled, tucking her earbuds away, allowing herself to hear the ambient sounds of the world around her.

As we walked together, I could see the determination in her step, but also the physical strain she was feeling. "My leg's acting up," she finally admitted. "I thought I could push through, but it's tougher than I expected." Without hesitation, I offered her one of my walking sticks.

"Are you sure?" she asked.

"I feel strong today," I assured her, and with that, she accepted the stick gratefully. We continued at a steady pace, talking about the challenges of the trail, our different reasons for walking the Camino, and the unexpected beauty we found along the way.

When we arrived at a small town for the midday stop, we parted ways for lunch. She ducked into a restaurant, while I wandered until I found a large table hosting some of the members of our Wind and Stars group, who were just finishing their meal. I nibbled on their leftover vegetable paella and some bread and cheese, keeping the meal light in order to save room for flan and cappuccino. I preserved very little energy for the next stretch of the journey.

After lunch, I walked with Maia, whose infectious laughter always lightened my mood and made the journey seem more playful. As we left the town, the path stretched out before us—a well-worn dirt trail, flanked by tall grasses that swayed in the gentle breeze. The scene felt timeless, as if the ancient shepherds and their flocks had carved the same path centuries before. The grasses brushed softly against my legs, their rustling a quiet accompaniment to our steps. The sun, now lower in the sky, cast a warm, golden glow, softening the afternoon's heat. The final miles of the day felt meditative, each step an opportunity to release the day's exertion. By the time we reached our hotel, my body hummed with sensations that were a satisfying reminder of the miles we'd conquered.

As the day's walk came to a close, I could feel the now familiar ache of fatigue in my muscles and also of something continuing to shift deep inside me—the ache of spiritual mending. Just as the earth below me bore the footprints of countless pilgrims before me, so did my body bear the stamp of my steps and so did my soul. I realized I was walking not just to cover distance but to stitch together parts of myself that had become frayed over time. The act of walking, step by step, mile after mile, was more than a journey of endurance. It was a gentle, but powerful, call to mend my life.

In the quiet of those last miles that day, I understood that the Camino wasn't just asking me to endure physical discomfort. It was inviting me to embrace small moments of grace—the offering of a walking stick, the symphony of birds and ocean, the kindness of strangers—and use them to bring together pieces of myself that had gotten scattered in the busyness of life.

This pilgrimage was my time to listen to the wind, to the earth, and to the soft inner voice calling me to continue onward, not just to the Cathedral at Santiago, but toward deeper healing.

Reflection Questions

How do you push through difficult moments when you feel like giving up? What keeps you moving forward?

When have you felt the support of a "Camino angel" or an unexpected helper for the journey of your life?

What sensory details can you notice today that ground you in the present moment?

How do you balance moments of solitude with connecting to others along your journey?

....

Ask a Better Question

*"Live the questions so that one day you will
live yourself into the answers."*

JACQUELINE NOVOGRATZ

The walk to Vila Praia de Âncora, which was a flat stretch along the Atlantic Ocean with secluded beaches and few tourists, felt familiar, akin to my experiences growing up on the East Coast of the United States. Here, I was greeted by white, sandy beaches and had plenty of sunlight left in the day to spread out my towel, soak up the salty air, and take a few cold plunges into the sea.

My body was in shock after the twelve-mile walk I mustered that day. I lost sight of the pilgrim's route when I was heading back to the seaside boardwalk, believing it would eventually lead me to my hotel.

But after walking miles out of the way, my legs tightened and refused to allow me to take another step forward.

I used the Bolt app on my phone to secure a taxi to take me the final mile into town. This was the answer to my first question of the walk: "How does the pilgrim experience look for me?"

After that initial experience of hitting the wall, I understood that I would listen to my body, push when needed, and give myself reprieve without judgment when necessary.

When I got back home, a close friend of over thirty years would ask, "What were you doing all day? Were you talking on the phone, using social media, or what?" She knew I had posted a two-minute video each day of the trip at 11:11 AM local time. But I explained that other than making this one post in the mornings, I was busy walking and it took all of my attention.

During the journey, there was a natural selection of groups that formed. There were the Power Walkers, who barely stopped to take a picture, the Cabinos, an untethered group of folks who spent leisurely mornings meandering the town and trail before riding to the next town in a taxi (the name was a fake Spanish word I made up for them meaning "people who joyfully take cabs"), and the SAS—short for Special Air Service—a group of five highly responsible folks who made a point of strolling through each town to ensure no one was ever left behind. One of their members was a British lady. Hence, the name.

The complex, yet simple nature of these few groups was a microcosm of what happens at home, work, and in the general flow of life. Some members of our larger group chose to walk solo, while others naturally moved freely between groups.

Being part of a walking group requires a certain amount of compromise—like waiting for slower-moving members when you want to speedwalk or committing to the day's plan even when you'd rather be lounging by the beach. I proudly identified as one of the older, slower members of the Power Walker clan. We weren't racing anyone, but we maintained a solid, steady pace and always arrived where we needed to be. Most afternoons, this group gathered for tapas and wine. I was grateful that nearly every restaurant in both Portugal and Spain offered cerveza sin 0.0 (non-alcoholic beer). Even without the alcohol, the brown bottle made a non-drinker feel more included.

Despite walking with nearly everyone in the group, there was one exception: a woman from Southern California whom my astrologer friend thought would be a great match for me. Almost immediately, my avoidance tactics went into full gear. We were staying in the same hotel overlooking the Douro River in Porto, and decided to meet for an early dinner. The conversation flowed easily— until she ordered a second glass of wine.

As soon as the second glass of wine appeared, my internal alarm sounded an alert, as familiar as an old friend at this point. My body tensed as if a gate was slamming shut, my thoughts sped up, and it took everything for me not to bolt from the table.

It's funny how things we think we keep hidden from the world are often obvious to others. Later, when I told this story to a longtime friend, we both laughed when she said she could picture my fidgeting leg bouncing nervously and eyes darting toward the door as I planned my exit strategy.

As someone committed to sobriety, I've made peace with friends who drink casually. But the thought of a partner who drinks regularly? *Nuh-uh.* That's a no-go for me.

Avoidance is my signature move, not just in relationships but with friendships too. I'm selective—probably *too selective*—about who gets into my inner circle. My emotional walls can be as solid as the ancient stone formations found along the Camino's Coastal Route. But this was exactly the kind of self-protection I had come to investigate on the pilgrimage. It was part of my inner journey.

The walk the day before, from the fishing town to the Hotel Monumento Convento in the Plaza de San Benito in A Guarda, Spain, while beautiful, was long. The scent of the ancient port reached me before I even saw the village. The salty tang of the ocean air mixed with the briny smell of fish carried on the breeze, a reminder that the sea was always close by. My steps grew heavier as the path transitioned from stony ground to dirt, putting a strain on my right foot and forming a blister on my heel. The muscles in my left inner thigh tightened with every step. When I finally arrived in town, only to learn that my hotel was at the top of the hill, I had a mini tantrum. Exhausted and aching, I refused to take another step, heading straight for the nearest restaurant along the harbor path.

Walking groups generally arrive in a town in time for a typical late lunch sometime between 1:30 PM and 3:00 PM. Most often, a few members of our group arrived at the same time, and we would gather for food and laughs. Because my body had given way on the long walk, and I insisted on eating at the harbor, I still had to endure a slow walk up the hill. With the help of a fellow traveler, I slowly inched my way up the white limestone stairs then followed the mosaic stone path toward the center of town.

Once at the hotel, I was pleasantly surprised to find a working bathtub in my room. After soaking for half an hour, I devoured what tasted like the most delicious Napoleon I'd ever eaten in my life. Just as the creamy custard soothed my mood, lying prone on the bed for several hours of rest eased the cramps in my legs. Once stores reopened for the evening, I found my way to a pharmacy for blister relief and sunscreen.

The next morning, I changed my shoes twice before leaving. It was Sunday, and the stone streets were empty and quiet. There were a few locals walking along the beach as I left town on my own for the second day in a row, and I stopped at the seaside park to make my 11:11 insight post while sitting on a swing. A few kilometers outside town, I came upon an ancient stone pool. To be with the experience and enjoy the gifts of the landscape, I decided to add steps, deviate from the trail, and go down the path toward the black, circular, volcanic rock structure perched beside the ocean.

As I drew closer, I could peer into the thick black walls of the structure, which reminded me of the subterranean kivas at Chaco Canyon in New Mexico, created by the ancestral Pueblo people. Inside, there were square clay structures resembling miniature dwellings. I found myself wondering, "Were these designed to catch fish?"

The sun began to peek through the clouds as a strong wind swept across the ancient site. I walked the full circumference of this prehistoric treasure, observing what appeared to be an old fishing or water filtration system. A nearby sign described it as "an impressive work of stone art that has withstood the test of time." Later, I discovered that this was an ancient fish trap, preserved through the centuries.

Interestingly, none of the other pilgrims from our group had ventured off the path to explore this hidden gem.

Given the choice, I've always been one to take the express train, going straight from point A to B without pausing to absorb the view or savor the experience. But on this day, I was grateful that I had decided to detour from my planned path to visit this ancient artifact. Taking the time to stop offered me a new perspective. Later, I learned that others in our group missed the trail turnoff and ended up walking a mile out of the way. Because I paused, I was able to spot other pilgrims heading up the hill from my vantage point on the rock—seeing the turn I might have easily missed if I had kept moving.

As I walked the Camino, I was purposely working to expand my pleasure in the moment by taking side streets and alternate routes, if possible, even when I knew that doing so would add steps to my day. I wanted to embrace the opportunities that the pilgrimage gave me for self-reflection.

As I stared into the curious pool of water below me, the wind began clearing my exhaustion. I was reminded of the story about unrequited love from Book 3 of Ovid's *Metamorphoses*. This is the tale of Narcissus, a beautiful youth, and Echo, the nymph who loves him deeply. Because Narcissus does not return her love, Nemesis, the daughter of Night and an avenging deity, punishes him by making him fall in love with his own reflection in a pool of water.

I reflected about the dinner several nights earlier on the patio overlooking Porto with the woman from my tour group. That interaction had served as a mirror to look more deeply at my habitual avoidance techniques and inability to commit fully to a partner. I welcomed my discomfort as an opportunity to form a better question about the relationships in my life.

As I gazed now at my aging reflection in the pool of ocean water, I asked myself, *What would it look like for me to be in a healthy, committed relationship?* There would be plenty of time to think about meaty questions like this one as I hobbled over the roots of trees and stone fragments left behind by the millions of pilgrims who had walked these same routes before me.

In my life, I am generally okay with myself. Even so, through asking questions that came up as I moved about in a community of peers within the context of a foreign land, I learned new information about myself and my relationships to the people I love. When I arrived home, I was able to make amends to my best friend for withholding love from her anytime I did not get what I thought I deserved or needed.

While walking that day, I realized that love is not a poker chip to throw on the table as an ante or to raise the stakes for the cards that I am holding in my hands.

Several days later, on the night before our final walk, I heard laughter coming from the lobby of the inn where everybody in the group was staying. I stood at the landing and surveyed my initial response, which was a feeling of disdain for people's laughter. Then I overcame my resentment for my own perception that I was "being left out of the fun" and headed down to join the group.

Soon I was laughing just as hard as the others were. We played Texas Hold 'Em, using potpourri as the source of our betting chits.

Not only was joining in the fun a personal win in moving forward from my self-defeating pattern of isolation, but by the end of the night I had also garnered a large pile of fragrant orange peels, rose petals, and cinnamon sticks. My clothes smelled wonderful after I tossed them into my luggage. That evening, I was more at ease with the woman from the rooftop patio who was seated to my right. I was not even paying attention to the wine consumption at the table because I was happy and felt connected.

Reflection Questions

What questions are you avoiding in your life, and what might happen if you started facing them?

How might you shift your perspective to gain new insights?

Is there anything you are not seeing about your current situation?

How could you be more open to the answers that come your way?

Are you willing to let down your guard?

....

Embrace Nonjudgmental Tolerance and Acceptance

"When we strive to become better than we are, everything around us becomes better too."

PAULO COELHO

In the heart of any transformative journey are the intertwined themes of nonjudgmental tolerance for others and self-acceptance. Both are acts of grace, often born from an ordeal that challenges our deeper faith and sense of meaning. There is nothing quite like traveling to another continent, state, or city to open our hearts and minds to people who are different from us.

Even venturing across our hometown can expose our prejudices and intolerance for differences, but traveling through another country where we ourselves are the foreigners helps us reflect more deeply, and humbly, on our preconceived notions. The diversity of experience and perspectives we encounter is an invigorating workout. Perhaps that's why I enjoyed exercising and expanding my ideas when up against the barriers of unfamiliar customs and languages along my pilgrimage, using the journey as an expression of my spiritual devotion.

In Paulo Coelho's acclaimed book *The Alchemist*, the journey of the protagonist, Santiago, exemplifies these themes, reminding us that acceptance can be a powerful ally in the quest to become more fully human. Santiago, like most of us, has preconceived notions of how others should live their lives, which are revealed through his journey. Melchizedek, the King of Salem, teaches Santiago that every person he meets is a reflection of himself and holds a piece of the truth he seeks. That idea strikes a chord in me.

During my pilgrimage on the Camino, I found myself in a similar position to Santiago. A Supreme Court decision back home in the United States that I applauded was not a consensus opinion within our small group of fourteen pilgrims, some of whom came from Canada and the United Kingdom. I quickly realized my reaction did not reflect the majority opinion. Like Santiago, I had to remain openminded and receptive to hearing the group's comments, to respect that their differing points of view came from a place of integrity within them. This experience taught me to shed my biases and walk with humility, understanding that every step taken is a step toward greater self-awareness and compassion.

In Portugal and Spain, dinner typically begins at 8 PM or later. As a weary walker, I often opted for a big lunch and skipped dinner. One night, after a particularly long day that required a late-afternoon rest, I ventured out later than usual. At 7:55 PM, the restaurant staff were still inside enjoying their preservice meal while I sat at an ocean-side patio table, waiting impatiently to be served. My judgmental mind couldn't help but wonder why, with so many pilgrims around, they didn't adjust their hours to accommodate them.

Soon, other diners began to fill up the tables around me, and I was joined by other pilgrims from my group. I quickly finished my meal. They lingered long after I left them to enjoy their wine and dine at leisure. From my open window in the room above the patio, I could hear their laughter as we all watched the magnificent sunset from our respective perches—me from the ocean-facing room I shared with a fellow group leader, and others from the beach below. The scene reminded me of the old saying "Red sky at night, sailor's delight." I drifted off to sleep, trusting that the next day's walk would unfold under a beautiful early summer sky.

Tolerance offers little space for the self-seeking behaviors of an entitled wanderer.

Most places we visited in Portugal welcomed travelers with a pilgrim's stamp for their Credencial and spoke Restaurant English. However, once we crossed the river into Spain, while vendors were hospitable, few spoke any English. It was therefore necessary for me to slow down and make more of an effort to be understood. A heartfelt smile with a thoughtful attempt to use the Google Translate app on my phone went a long way when seeking sunscreen at the pharmacy. I ultimately learned that the same patience required to walk alone for hours day after day is essential for deepening your experience as a pilgrim when you are among people. Expanding your awareness to embrace another person's point of view when making a connection is the key.

The inability to speak and understand the language in each country limits the experience and shapes your perspective. Looking around at mealtime, I was often envious of entrées on the plates at the next table over from mine. I would have been better served at dinner and elsewhere if I'd had more humility throughout my life and realized that English is not the only language worth learning. I must reluctantly admit that despite all my years of traveling in Peru and elsewhere, I have not made much of an effort to study foreign tongues. My arrogance was now coming back to haunt me.

A language barrier can provide another mirror to shed light on our similarities and differences. Aha moments are as plentiful as the cobblestones lining the village streets. A cranky English-speaking pilgrim can turn even a hospitable Spaniard sour. A quick pivot in expectations and the realization that it was my responsibility, as the foreigner in Spain, to communicate in a way that others could under-stand, shifted this dynamic. I also had to forgive myself for my limitations.

Throughout my pilgrimage to Compostela, I encountered numerous opportunities to practice nonjudgmental tolerance of others and self-acceptance. From the diverse range of opinions within our small group on social and political issues to the cultural richness of the places we visited, experiencing the fullness of each moment in a community became a lesson in seeing beyond appearances and embracing our shared humanity.

For the most part, the members of our Wind and Stars travel group were well-suited companions. Conversations at community meals were charged with descriptions of our accomplishments, infectious laughter, inside jokes, playful teasing, and flow. Loud banter always filled the room.

Still, as in any group that is faced with the daunting task of walking 118 miles, normal wear and tear can give rise to a kind of disenchantment that is both physical and emotional. As fatigue set in, small irritations became magnified. The collective strain of moving from town to town brought out some underlying tensions along the way. I had to keep myself in check when a fellow traveler left my walking stick at the hotel, with seemingly little regard for the sacrifice I made on my own physical comfort to loan it to her. All was forgiven when the transport company circled back to the hotel's reception area, picked up the stick and delivered it with the luggage the next day.

In our customarily jovial travel pod, conflicting opinions began to form about the exclusivity of small groups, organizational leadership, and the lack of walking participation by the Cabinos. One evening, fueled by too much wine, social tension and the hurt feelings of a few younger members led to some heightened verbal banter about these topics while we noshed on tapas in a local pub. Their disenchantment culminated in what felt like a psychic attack on the rest of us.

In any human context, gossip and negativity are often birthed, then magnified, through exhaustion, frustration, judgments, and preconceived notions.

Along the way in *The Alchemist,* Santiago meets himself through his interactions with many human mirrors. For example, there is a crystal merchant who seems "stagnant" in his life. But when Santiago can transform his opinions about the merchant's lack of ambition, he is able to work alongside him for positive change. My companions and I needed to take a page from that book.

We live in a time of polarization, where it is easy to forget that we are all connected through the winds of breath and experience. If we are open pilgrims, walking the Camino will break down the rubber on the shoes of our judgment. Pilgrimage can provide the walker an opportunity to see beyond appearances and shift perspectives on others and themselves.

The inspiration to post daily Instagram reels at 11:11 AM came before I left for Europe. My friend Don Deffendorf shared that he longed to walk but was physically unable. He sent me the book *Walking Home* to read in preparation for the journey, and I promised to pray for him daily on my walk. Because all of this took place over email, I didn't know that he was sick.

Following the trip, I realized that Don's quiet generosity of spirit, which contributed to my 11:11 insights, was offered during his final days on earth. Don passed away, walking home to Spirit, while I was in Europe. The day he passed, I began my walk to Pontevedra, unaware of his transition. However, I did notice a tile marker bearing the number 11 on the side of a stone house, signifying new beginnings.

Many people, including my mom, shared that the Camino was a trip they wished they could've taken. While many are called (or at least intrigued by the prospect), not everyone can endure the physically demanding walk. I wanted to include them in my journey, so I committed to creating a video each day in which I shared an insight gleaned from the pilgrimage experience.

My first video was shot in Porto, late in the afternoon, with a sunset backdrop of colorful laundry as vivid as the azulejo, the Portuguese, blue-toned patterned tile covering many walls in this ancient city. Coming from the United States, where wet laundry is dried inside a machine, I looked upon the clotheslines in awe and wonder.

Every home on the block had pulley clotheslines strung off the kitchen balcony, with laundry flapping proudly in the constant breeze of the busy street. The wind reminded me to hunt for the name of the Portuguese wind spirit that filled these sheets and shirts with life. Then my judgmental and intolerant mind wandered into the past, recalling my grandmother's banter about not hanging dirty laundry out to dry. For her, it meant no one should ever see the dysfunction behind the walls of our home or hers, lest they look down on our family. But here in Porto, people hung their well-worn garments, underwear, and stained bedding from the iron balconies for all passersby, including me, to witness and wonder.

Once the pilgrim's walk began in earnest, I had to focus on the business at hand: walking. To keep my video journaling commitment, I recorded my reflections about my pilgrimage and what I was learning from it within minutes of leaving the hotel each day. The iPhone photo app became a reliable companion, capturing the dated history of every stop, favorite site, and the accompanying remarks. The camera stored hundreds of pictures and videos—my windspirations.

Windspirations, a term coined by a fellow member of the Wind Clan, a community formed around my book *Winds of Spirit*, describes the insights received in nature, particularly those delivered by the wind. A few years earlier, I wrote this book about wind gods and goddesses from cultures around the world, and since then, the movement of air has become a constant force and focus for me, directing my life.

Keeping a steady gait was the best way for me to walk. Slowing down would make the hills seem taller and could turn ten miles into eternity. If I found myself moving like a turtle, I would restart my pace by joining the momentum of other pilgrims.

After Vigo, there was a convergence of pilgrims from all the Camino trails. Behind me during one video I made in our second week in Spain, you can see a steady stream of walkers and a farmhouse with a red-tiled roof. At this point in the journey, it was hard to find my pace amid the commotion of more walkers. The trail felt crowded and noisy after my long walks with myself in nature. A particular annoyance was the sound of walking sticks without rubber tips on limestone, which was slick from dew.

The terrain on the route to Santiago alternates between ancient rocks, modern pavement, and compacted soil, depending on location. My favorites were earthen paths through forest, where I was surrounded by fragrant eucalyptus trees.

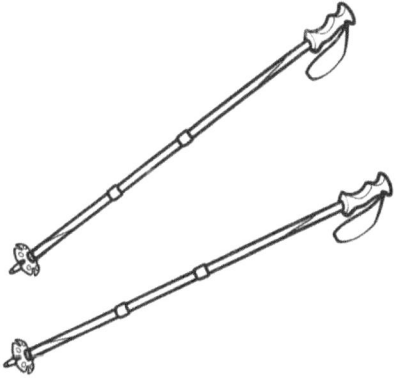

For the entire day, I ran ahead of groups or waited to fall behind them to regain my moments of peace and quiet in the wooded areas. I even found myself cursing and judging those people who would walk with their sticks tapping the metal rhythmically on the stone.

By mid-morning, when I reached Alba, there was a beautiful chapel, the Capilla de San Cayetano. Inside, it was full of noisy pilgrims vying for places in line to self-stamp their Camino passports. Despite the ruckus at the back of the small chapel, I managed to sit and pray, asking for patience with the trail commotion, especially pilgrims who walked with metal-tipped hiking poles that went clickity-clack on the cobblestones in town.

Upon leaving this small town, I wandered through some abandoned vineyards. Stone pillars, weathered by centuries of wind and rain, stood proudly among the decaying vines. In my mind, I also wandered through my own story about how these ancient supports, crafted from the region's native stone, are a testament to both the vineyard's long history and the millions of pilgrims who have passed by it. Like these pillars, pilgrims are unique, bearing their own marks of time, similar to the cracks, moss, and lichen that add character to the pillars and give them a sense of timelessness. There is time, when walking solo, to imagine the stories of people who have tended the land. I even wondered if these abandoned fields had caretakers, and why, with wine being as popular as it is, so many fields in this region were being left untilled.

Before I could get buried too deeply in that thought, once again the landscape changed, and I found myself heading up a path into a forest. As I was climbing a hill into the trees, I spied Liz, another solo walker from my group, ahead of me. She was kind and paced her day with mine from then on. We stopped late in the morning for a drink at A Pousada do Peregrino. The café we visited was packed with other pilgrims, including the Power Walkers from our group, who were just finishing their snacks and heading back onto the trail. Tuckered out by many days of exertion, my patience was wearing thin with all the noise we encountered in the village.

I encouraged us to stop for rest one too many times, and my thighs gave out miles before the next town came into sight. We ended up taking a taxi to the next stop. I reconciled this decision by acknowledging that the ten noisy miles I had pushed myself through that day were enough, and that listening to my body was important. Even though we seemed to be in the middle of nowhere most of the time while hiking, a cab is always only ten minutes away.

The taxi driver kindly stopped at the Parque Natural del Rio Barosa, a scenic enclave that features a beautiful waterfall surrounded by rocks. Other pilgrims were splashing around in the pool at the base of the falls. Although I was too tired to remove my shoes, I was grateful that the driver had brought us to witness this magical force of nature—a sight I would have missed had we continued on foot, as it added more than a mile to an already long day.

Looking back, I am amazed that even halfway through the hundred-mile-plus trail, I was still bargaining with myself—finding excuses to reward myself with extra hours in the Caldas de Reis hot springs, the destination for that day's walk. Caldas de Reis, nestled in a quiet corner of Galicia along the Umia River, is a small town that serves as a key stop on the Portuguese route to Santiago de Compostela. The town's rich history is intertwined with its natural thermal springs, a refuge for weary pilgrims dating back to the Middle Ages. The name itself translates to "Hot Water of the Kings."

We stayed at the somewhat dated Caldas de Reis Spa Hotel, which featured a large outdoor thermal pool. While the accommodations were just adequate and the breakfast unremarkable, the spa treatment was exceptional. There were also outdoor pools along the riverbanks near the hotel where pilgrims could be seen soaking their feet and muscles to recuperate after long days of walking.

Throughout the afternoon, other walkers from the Wind and Stars group trickled into the large rectangular pool to soak, nap, laugh, and reconnect. After a rejuvenating soak, I joined my walking companion Liz for a pilgrim's special meal at Cafeteria Termas, just across the bridge from our hotel. The riverside cafe was packed with walkers enjoying *cervezas*. I was particularly grateful that nearly every place in Portugal and Spain offered alcohol-free beer.

The three-course early-bird menu began with croquettes or a large plate of ham, followed by a choice of mains. I opted for a simple chicken scallopini with vegetables, while Liz chose salmon. Feeling content and full, I limped back to my chaise longue and lay by the pool until it was time for a much-anticipated spa treatment.

This was not the first time I found myself judging my decisions during the trek. My self-criticism pounded down on me like the cascading waterfall I had visited earlier that day. I was easily anguished by decisions about whether to spend an extra day at the beach, visit a spa for a massage, or take a taxi. Whether walking alone or with another, it soon became apparent to me that, in my life, the harshest judgments I hold are always aimed at myself, only to be reflected outward.

During our walk, the weather was mostly sunny and moderate, but one day brought the looming threat of rain. Prepared with my rain poncho the next morning, I set off toward Padron, Spain, feeling ready for whatever the weather might throw my way. We started along the ancient Roman road, Via Romana XIX, which had been built nearly two millennia ago. As we crossed the Bermaña River Bridge, I marveled at its semicircular arches, remnants of the old pavement still visible. Carved into one side of the stone bridge was a medieval cross, quietly watching over the centuries of pilgrims who had passed by. After a restorative afternoon soaking in thermal springs and indulging in a much-needed massage, I began my day feeling revitalized and ready to broadcast my 11:11 insight.

I paused to record a reel on the judgments we hold against ourselves and others. Tension was bubbling up within our travel group. Some walkers felt excluded, and the Cabinos were being criticized for not fully engaging in the walk. When I learned that one of our group members had tossed away the white cap I had gifted her at our first dinner, I felt a pang of personal hurt.

She casually remarked, "I am not one of them," a dismissal that stung more than I expected.

Objectively, we were going through the natural phases of group dynamics—*forming, storming,* and eventually, *norming*—but I realized I was harboring my own growing judgments. As I asked myself how judgment was showing up in my life, I saw clearly how my external critiques mirrored the self-judgment and criticism I often directed inward. The tensions within our group only highlighted the personal work I needed to do, reminding me to soften my view both of others and of myself.

About thirty minutes into the walk, I lazily pulled my walking sticks from my pack without stopping to remove it from my back. As I adjusted the pole length, I realized that one of my walking sticks had lost its rubber tip. I now had a clicking stick. Every time my pole hit the rocky path for the rest of the trip, this profound trick of Spirit reminded me of just how judgmental I can be.

Once you bring awareness to a topic, Spirit seems to conspire to provide fuel for your flame. As I walked on, I saw a man in the woods. Judgment surfaced again. He looked like a tall leprechaun, with a cane, a cap, and a mischievous smile. Suddenly, I questioned the ease with which I had been walking alone—*Should I be cautious or at least more aware?*

As my leisurely pilgrim self-meandered on, I heard a barrage of gunfire in the distance, immediately heightening my senses. Working farms surrounded me, with open spaces stretching between me and the next grove of trees. *Is someone hunting?* Soon, I emerged from the fields into the small town of O Cruceiro, where a small marching band paraded across my path. I identified the source of the shots I'd heard: a twenty-one-gun salute.

Shaken by the sudden turn of events, I stopped at Esperón, a café and bar serving pilgrims, where I used the bathroom in exchange for a purchase of a cappuccino that I didn't end up drinking.

This important lesson about intolerance has stuck with me. Now I carry in my mind my click sticks of judgment. While other pilgrims left their walking sticks in the certification office in Santiago because the trip was done, I decided to carry my metal pole home as a reminder to stay in my own lane of tolerance and acceptance mentally.

Reflection Questions

How does it feel to become aware of your inner judgments throughout the day?

What types of judgments do you find yourself making most often? Are they directed more at yourself, others, or situations?

Have you noticed patterns in your judgments?

What underlying beliefs or fears might be fueling your judgments?

How does it feel in your body and mind when you let go of a judgment? What replaces that feeling?

Are you willing to practice nonjudgmental tolerance and acceptance in your daily life?

....

Drop the Should-Haves, Could-Haves, and Would-Haves

"Never regret anything that made you smile."

ATTRIBUTED TO MARK TWAIN

Decades ago, I used to batter my partner with not-so-helpful statements like "Relationships are supposed to be . . ." To which she would respond, "What page of *The Relationship Handbook* is that on?" My self-righteous belief in life coming with a set of rigid rules and guidelines like those that could be found in a book has been the undoing of me and my peace many times throughout my life.

In time, I learned that I'd have better relationships if I had fewer expectations of people. On the Camino, I found out that this goes for being a pilgrim as well. Going to Compostela is a personal journey, and it was not up to me to be the teacher who grades another. Each of us gets to choose about walking, biking, cabbing, using metal points on our poles (or not), and even not walking.

Before heading out on the journey, as is my pattern, I was very busy. I bought my plane ticket without studying the maps, hotels, and the towns we would visit. For much of my life, I've planned trips within an inch of their lives, leaving little room for grace and the possibility of change. This time the tour operator provided the outline. The only requirement of me after helping to fill the trip with pilgrims was to show up for dinner the nights the group gathered, open a wind space, call in a wind spirit for each walker, and close the space at our final group dinner. Other than that, I was free to dance in the winds of Spirit.

Millions of pilgrims have moved along the trails of the Camino de Santiago throughout the centuries because it is considered a place of spiritual power. These routes are ley lines, forming a kind of energy map of the land in the region. There are many places like this, with engrained power, throughout the world, including Stonehenge, the Pyramids of Giza, Machu Picchu, and perhaps even unexpected places near your own home. I have been on several pilgrimages in my life when I was feeling thirsty for spiritual guidance; by following a sacred path along a ley line I have experienced a quickening of my awakening and received deep guidance and insight.

Following a visit to Stonehenge, a friend and I visited Bath in Somerset. We both felt ill at ease the entire stay, and when we entered one of the famed bathhouses, I immediately got sick to my stomach. I felt better as we drove away from the town. I had another purging experience after a ceremony one evening on the sacrificial death stone in Machu Picchu. After a sleepless night lying on the bathroom floor between bouts of vomiting, my teacher came in, looked me up and down, and said, "Your chakras are now running clear."

Places of power have unique lessons to share when we accept the invitation to visit.

Setting an intention is a personal experience that generally begins once we say yes to the trip, or even before we do, because we have a predetermined date with destiny. Maneuvering while you call forth a spiritual experience may bring roadblocks, obstacles, synchronicities, and miracles.

Most mornings, the larger group would gather for breakfast before heading out to find the first yellow arrow at 8:30 AM. If the Cabinos planned to walk that day, they would first drop their luggage at the registration desk, then return to their morning meditations, business activities, beach strolls, or walks in the woods nearby. They would choose a desirable late-morning starting point, typically closer to the next town, and then cab to that spot.

There was a trickster amid this group, the woman I refer to in this book as Loki, who invited me nightly not to walk the next day, but instead to rest, recover, and take a taxi with them. The spiritual gift of tricksters is known to me as Coyote medicine. The aim is to help people shed rigidity, reverse the order, to allow flow and laughter. Each day I had to look deeper inside to find my reason to carry on walking despite the temptation to stop.

As I watched the Cabinos laughing over a glass of wine every evening, I couldn't help but compare my aching feet and blisters to their relaxed, joyful state. *Maybe they've got it figured out,* I thought. *Maybe my determination to walk every mile is just stubbornness dressed up as spiritual commitment.* The doubt gnawed at me, and I found myself questioning whether my way was the "right" way after all.

In 2004, I entered a two-year healer's training program. I evaluated my spiritual gifts (or the lack thereof), by comparing my ability to take a shamanic journey to one of the worlds of Spirit accompanied by the steady sound of a drumbeat to the ability of other members of the group. In my estimation, my fellow students were reporting having had more vivid, stronger, and clearer visioning experiences than I did during these repetitive drum exercises. Had it not been for the prodding of the teacher to continue and a spontaneously experienced "dismemberment" that came later, my low self-esteem would have pushed me to the sidelines of my intended path.

One day the phone rang, and the woman on the other end said, "I hear you are a shaman." In disbelief of my own abilities, I resisted helping her at first, before agreeing to her request. Even so, somewhere deep inside me I knew I had to answer the growth call, and I went to work helping others.

The need to prove myself socially has been a lifelong obsession, dating back to elementary school. This pursuit of external approval started early— each new classroom after a move meant I had to prove I was likable and capable. Despite my protests, teachers would often place me with the slow learners, and I had to fight to prove I belonged. That drive to secure my place wasn't something I was ready to let go of, even now.

Despite years of trying to learn self-acceptance, on the Camino I still found myself needing validation from my companions, especially as an aging woman. I felt old, fat, and worn out.

Even though my feet staged nightly protests, I refused to give in to the temptress Loki. She dangled promises of shorter walks, shopping sprees, and sightseeing. Every time, her playful invitations nudged the part of me that longed for ease, but I kept resisting. It wasn't just about walking the miles; it was about proving something deeper to myself. As I limped along, trying to keep up with the younger, more agile walkers, I felt a surge of inadequacy. Their footsteps seemed lighter, faster, as if they barely touched the ground. My own pace felt slow, heavy, and with each step, I could feel the creeping comparisons taking root in my mind: *Why can't I move like them? Am I even cut out for this pilgrimage?*

We often laughed until we were winded—the kind of laughter that comes when you know each other's quirks all too well. Loki's playful persistence was part of stimulating that laughter, but it also stirred up something within me that wanted healing. Each time she offered the easy way out, I had to pause and wonder, *What am I really here for?* The issue I was wrestling with wasn't just about how I handled the physical walk; it was about shedding old rules I didn't even realize I was still following.

As we laughed, I felt my arms open just a little wider. Maybe Loki wasn't just tempting me with ease, but with a chance to step out of my own expectations. *Am I comparing my journey to others'? And if so, why?* I mused.

The Camino mirrored these questions back to me. As I walked, the nagging doubts surfaced: *Is there a right way to do this journey? Am I clinging to self-imposed rules out of the fear of doing it wrong? Can those who walk every mile claim more spiritual favor than those who choose a lighter, more relaxed path?* Each step was a reflection of the expectations I carried—both of myself and others—and how easily those expectations could weigh me down, just like the physical strain of the walk itself.

Just like the times I walked past a yellow arrow, distracted by my inner dialogue of comparisons and should-haves, I realized how easy it is to miss the signs pointing the way forward. These markers, simple yet vital, were my reminders to trust the path even when I couldn't see beyond the next bend. Each clamshell etched into the stone was an invitation to stop, recalibrate, and remember that the journey itself was the destination—just like in life. Any time we're too focused on our expectations or comparisons, we can miss the subtle guidance that shows up along the way.

The yellow arrows and clamshells on the Camino reminded me that the path is always there, even when I'm unsure of the next step. They called me to pay attention, to trust that the way forward would reveal itself if I stayed open and aware.

In my book *Winds of Spirit,* there is a story about Vayu, the Vedic wind god who rules the space between the sun and earth, and Vasuki, the snake god. Both considered themselves to be the most powerful, all-knowing force in the universe and set off to have a competition to prove their prowess and strength. Vasuki wrapped himself around Mount Meru three times, and Vayu blew his breath full force to uncoil him. As Vayu blew harder, the mountain swayed, and Vasuki tightened his grip. Mount Meru ordered them to cease their battle lest he tumble into the sea and put an end to civilization.

The creator god Brahma appeased Vayu and Vasuki by praising their virtues as equally powerful.

Each path along the Camino would require me to be equally brave. I had to become clear about my choice. I came to walk. Despite the blisters on my feet and my muscles that tightened like a crank had been wound, I persevered, because like Vasuski, walking was the coiled rope that tethered my experience. Over and again, I was tested as Vayu shook at the itinerary and I was confronted to extract my real preferences and purpose.

When we were at Hotel Attica 21, Wellness and Spa, there was an option to stay for a second night instead of moving inland to the city of Pontevedra, Spain, as planned. There was a free, non-walking day in our schedule. The Cabino Babes were very clear: They were staying put. My body, heart, and soul wanted to spend another day with them, still my obligation to the rest of the group and the planned move to Pontevedra surfaced. I tossed and turned into the night trying to summon the courage to say out loud to the group that I wanted to stay put. To my surprise, when I phoned the front desk to book the extra night, the clerk said, "The charge comes to one-hundred and eleven Euros, madame."

As a group leader, it was not until more members of the group began to stray from the agenda, indicating their decisions to stay put, that I texted Victoria and expressed my truth. The social proof of others sharing my sentiment granted me the permission to stay behind with the majority.

Walking helped me realize I never missed an opportunity, hypothetical scenarios do not serve me, and conditional realities only exist in my imagination. It was time to stop comparing my choices and gifts with the choices and gifts of others. While I could accept others doing as they wished, I was not yet granting myself the same freedom.

Fortunately, there were no should-haves on our Camino expedition. The Camino had the answers that everyone's soul sought.

On a side note, in the end, one participant who cabbed as much as she walked during the entire journey got to experience her own special aha moments while engaged in a duel with COVID. She had a high fever for four days following our arrival at the imaginary finish line in Compostela. I was relieved that I did not get similarly sick.

Spirit will always give us the medicine we invite when we decide to become a pilgrim on any journey. Walk or do not walk. To say yes to the Camino is to invite in the wisdom of all the ancient souls that have walked before you.

In the end, for me the only worthwhile comparison on the journey was the one between who I had been until then and who I was becoming. It wasn't about proving my worth through miles walked or lessons learned; it was about embracing the moment, releasing my need for comparison, and honoring who I had become along the way.

Reflection Questions

What rigid beliefs or expectations do you find yourself holding on to, and how can you begin to let them go?

In what ways have you found yourself comparing your journey to that of others?

How can you focus on your personal growth instead of seeking external validation?

What simple shift can you make to embrace your unique journey without judgment?

How have your expectations shaped your past experiences, and how might you release control to allow more flow in the future?

INSIGHT EIGHT

···

Rest Is Essential

"Take rest; a field that has rested gives a bountiful crop."

OVID

For me, walking the Camino was an exploration of what it would be like to stop working, and an opportunity to connect deeper with myself spiritually. I hoped it would help me to organize the next stage of my life. Throughout my life, I have always found it necessary to isolate myself and step away from my busy daily routines to remember my oneness with nature. Intention is key, and once a decision is made to separate myself and take a rest from mundane experiences, Spirit always opens the visionary door. I knew undertaking a pilgrimage would require prayer, communicating with Spirit, and gathering strength and knowledge.

As you know, two nights before our group gathered to officially begin our experience in late May, I had a dream about a bear. Then, a month after I returned from Europe, I had another dream, which, when I recorded it in my dream log, revealed a forgotten dream that had occurred weeks before I embarked on the journey.

In the first forgotten dream of the series, a bear was stretched out on a picnic table in what I recognized as the food barn at Camp Bonnie Brae, the sleepaway camp I attended at age seven. My cat Sami was also in the dream, frozen by my side as we both sensed the powerful presence of the larger mammal. I misplaced this dream memory until I was searching for the details of a second bear dream that occurred the first night in Portugal, after waking from that third dream. My record of that second dream is one of two written entries in my travel journal because I got it soaking wet the next day!

That night in July, I woke up shaken after a vivid third encounter with the bear in my dreams. Jolted awake by my heavy breathing, I could feel my heart pounding as I sensed the bear's urgency, its sharp claw reaching through the crack of the door. The bear was getting closer still.

Bear sightings, both literal and in dreams, have dotted my life in moments when it was soon going to make a pivotal turn in a new direction. Twenty-five years before, when I was walking along the dips and climbs of a hill with a holy man, going out to begin a vision quest, he asked me, "Have you ever seen a bear?" Imagine my fear when the elder who was going to leave me in my *sacred hoop,* an area on the ground about the size of a queen-sized bed, protected from the elements only by a simple strand of red, white, black, and yellow ties that I'd woven, said this.

It had taken me months to complete those ties, interweaving them with my prayers and a tobacco mix. Now I was going to be alone with myself and a *chanupa* (Lakota Sioux ceremonial pipe), singing songs and praying prayers for three days and two nights in an unfamiliar forest on Los Coyotes Reservation.[1] The holy man's question set the sacred stage for this time of inward reflection, by planting the image of a bear in my mind.

At nightfall, I would imagine how I would respond if a bear should come out from the brush of tightly woven shrubs. My camp, while set in a clearing, appeared to be protected from hikers or anyone else who might be wandering through the dense high desert forest. Although I did not see a bear during my vision quest, my active imagination dreamed I did. Still, the bear became an important spirit totem in my life.

A few years after this *haŋbléčeyapi* ("crying for a vision") ceremony, I went on a different kind of pilgrimage to the Vermont Studio Center to paint. For a month, I had a faceoff with myself. This time, there was an untethered schedule, a studio space, and large canvases spanning the walls. The center was miles into the wilderness near the Canadian border, which provided generous trails through the woods, rivers to canoe, and hours alone in my painting studio—womb-like hibernation. By the end of the month, I had painted many large canvases filled with colorful nature forms of bears, doing all kinds of mundane activities from rowing a boat to doing an old Norse rune spread.

Before, during, and after the trip, my days were packed full, so the bear was stalking me at night in my dreams, where he could get my full attention. The bear's presence evoked a memory of a past-life journey where, upon entering a cave unsuspectingly, a grizzly bear dismembered me: I was taken apart piece by piece.

Today, whenever I see a bear or think of a bear, it reminds me that I'm being dismembered and put back together again. I trust that the chaos I'm undergoing inside is driven by instinct, self-determination, and love, rather than self-sabotage or a malicious external force of some kind.

During the pilgrimage, my need to keep busy was being dismantled, and I was beginning to value rest. I was taught this lesson many times during the trip. Rest is an essential part of the awakening experience.

Midway through the Camino, our group took a day off at a luxury hotel outside Vigo that offered gourmet food and had a state-of-the-art spa. (This is the place I told you about in Insight Six.) This sleek modern hotel faced Samil Beach, which has a boardwalk that extends for miles and features restaurants, gelato stands, and white sand. This would be our final coastal hotel before the Camino path turned inland at the metropolitan center of Vigo, the most populated city in the northwestern region of Galicia. Since entering Spain a few days earlier, we had been in the Pontevedra province.

It takes a week to walk a pilgrim's path that a car can cover in a few hours. To put it into perspective, the distance from Porto to Santiago de Compostela is roughly the same as the stretch of highway from Palm Springs to Los Angeles—about 106 miles. When we reached the coastal hotel, as you know, many of us opted for an extra day of rest. The Atlantic waters and the healing spa were a welcome break, reminding me that rest is not just a physical necessity but an act of self-compassion. While others pressed on, I understood that, sometimes, slowing down is the most courageous step you can take.

My companions and I spent hours enjoying the multifunctional water jets in the spa, letting the aches in our limbs dissolve in the soothing waters. After debating whether to stick to the itinerary or indulge in an extra day by the ocean, I had chosen rest. My body thanked me. The comfortable bed, the attentive housekeeping, and the refreshing Atlantic breeze were more than just physical comforts; they offered much-needed recovery. Plus, it was fun spending time with others in our group who chose to take this pause, walking at a different beat from the usual hurried pace of the pilgrimage.

Each of us had our little comforts to keep us going, whether it was herbal salves or cherished snacks. One fellow walker joked that out of the ten-plus pounds in her backpack, it was a roll of toilet paper that she prized most. This became a running joke among us: What were we willing to lug around, not out of necessity, but because it brought us some peace of mind? In many ways, those comfort items, though small, felt essential to the experience.

Our tour organizer, Victoria, called us "high maintenance." She teased us about our luggage on the very first day and even more so when we decided to stay behind for an extra night at the spa. As one by one, the pilgrims opted for rest over putting on more mileage, it became a domino effect. Nine of us stayed behind while five—mostly Power Walkers—continued on. We reminded Victoria that this was preventative maintenance. Sometimes, giving in to comfort is exactly the self-care needed to keep going.

Even without walking herself, Victoria got healing on the trip. She was confronted daily with her desire to be a good guide. Due to the balancing act she made with wine, perfectionism, and control, she lost her patience with us many times. We required a loosening of the itinerary grip that was hard for her. With so many pilgrims walking the trail, the logistics of smoothly moving luggage from town to town and having limited three- and four-star hotels to choose from along the route had taken her months of advanced planning.

Still, organizing an amazing itinerary can lock in the experience in advance. But ours was a group of rugged individualists who would say, "Don't worry, I'll get my luggage and myself there." We were marching according to the force of our own winds. Lost luggage was always found, and even my walking stick, which I loaned to someone who left it behind, caught up to me at the next hotel.

In nature, there is a time for rest. Farmers understand that in some years a field needs to be turned and left unplanted, so its nutrients can be restored. Like leaving a field fallow, resting is not an optional part of any walking pilgrimage. At the end of each day's trek, I would literally lie out on my bed for an hour until my legs stopped throbbing from walking and the muscles moved back into harmony with my feet. During the journey, I also had several massages. I was learning that Spirit does not judge the merits of pilgrims who push forward as worse than the merits of those who rest.

For me, real reconciliation with the idea of resting came when I first gave myself permission to stop. Along the Camino, I encountered many stone markers and yellow arrows, guiding my every step forward. These simple symbols reassured me that I was on the right path. Yet, the same markers that urged me onward also reminded me that rest was a part of the journey, not a detour from it.

There were three times during the journey when I made a hard and fast stop. The first time, I chose to take a cab for the last mile into town, with my friend from London, who was also worn down.

The second time, I missed one of those ever-present arrows and got lost, walked miles out of the way, until I literally could not lift my leg to take one more step forward. Since I was hiking by the shore, I went for a swim in the ocean. Taking periodic dips in the brisk Atlantic waters the rest of that day gave me the impetus to walk on.

The third time, I chose to rest many times along the trail before catching a cab to visit hot, mineral water pools.

On all three occasions, resting made me a stronger pilgrim.

After I returned from Europe, I felt an undeniable need for more rest. My body was weary, and my sleep patterns were out of sync. It was a clear reminder that physical recovery is essential for spiritual renewal. Just as the Camino had demanded endurance, my body now demanded restoration.

I listened, slowly rebuilding my energy. I found myself falling asleep early, only to dream of walking. It turns out, rest isn't just physical—it's a full-body reset, including the mind.

In a world that pushes us to keep moving, we often neglect the importance of true rest. But if bears can hibernate for months without guilt, surely we can allow ourselves the space to recharge, right? Bears don't sleep for fun. They're storing energy for the future, preparing for the adventures to come.

While I lay in bed, thinking of all the things I "should" be doing, I realized that my brain was like a bear; it needed downtime after the Camino to gear up for the next phase of my life's journey.

When I finally began rising well before dawn each day, aligning with the time zone in Europe, I felt energized and ready to write and share my experiences from the journey. Yet, my body still craved extra sleep to fully process the experience. I would be in bed before dark and rise before sunlight. One morning, as I looked in the mirror, I saw a face staring back at me that was well-rested, with clear, bright eyes—a sign that I was finally replenishing my energy.

Bears hibernate during the winter, conserving energy for the coming spring. My rest phase felt similar, as I conserved energy after the pilgrimage. In a world where society faces constant threats and challenges, like climate change, pandemics, and polarization, self-care is essential for balance and well-being. Like the essential stored fat that sustains a hibernating bear, rest is our essential "fat." It sustains us and keeps us well. Throughout Native American history, the elders often turned to the bear for guidance. When bears kept appearing to me in dreams before and during the Camino, I believe they were teaching me to respect the natural rhythms of my life, including honoring my need to rest, just as they and the earth rest during winter.

I was reminded of this bear wisdom each day on our walk when I would pass the *hórreos,* structures which almost every home in Galicia has. These granite, concrete, or wooden-roofed structures on stilts are used to store corn or grain after the fall harvest. Just as the hórreos protect and preserve the harvest for future use, ensuring that the community has sustenance through the winter, the bear's hibernation preserves its energy for the cold months ahead. These symbols of preservation and preparation serve as daily reminders of the importance of gathering and conserving our inner resources, whether it be food, energy, or wisdom, to nourish ourselves through times of rest and renewal.

History keeps track. In the Greek myth of Persephone, the daughter of Demeter (the goddess of agriculture and harvest), is kidnapped by Hades, the god of the underworld. Grief stricken and desperate to find her daughter, Demeter neglects her duties, causing the earth to become barren and lifeless. No crops grow, and the land falls into a deep state of famine. Zeus, the king of the gods, sees the suffering of humanity and intervenes, commanding Hades to release Persephone. However, before letting her go, Hades tricks Persephone into eating pomegranate seeds, binding her to the underworld for a part of each year.

This story explains how important it is for us to honor the natural cycles of growth and rest. The barren winter months, like the quiet introspection of a pilgrimage, represent a time of rest and recuperation for us. Just like the earth, rest is necessary to ensure the vibrant growth and abundance that come later with spring and summer. A pilgrimage can teach us that rest is an integral part of nature's cycle, ensuring our renewal and sustainability.

Having unscheduled times when the demands of the world are not pulling on our "strings," as if we're marionettes, is vital to our well-being. Even if we cannot take a long pilgrimage or vacation, it is crucial to carve out space to take walks, do hobbies, cook a meal with friends, or engage in other activities that we love. This unwinding may feel unnatural at first, but as we allow the process to unfold, we find more joy and possibility for meaning.

Reflection Questions

How does your body communicate its need for rest? Do you listen to these internal signals?

Have you ever pushed on despite your body saying "stop"?

How do you currently make time for rest?

What does rest look like to you?

What activities help you unwind and reconnect with yourself?

How can you embrace periods of rest without feeling guilty or unproductive?

Are there any wild adventures in your future for which you are storing your energy?

INSIGHT NINE

....

Sing a Song

"A bird doesn't sing because it has an answer. He sings because he has a song."

JOAN WALSH ANGLUND

Laughter is a balm for the soul. There is nothing more soothing after a long day on the trail than a giggle that turns into a full-on belly laugh. We laughed and squealed with joy throughout the pilgrimage and found it lightened the heavy load of our packs, expectations, and worn-out bodies.

One night I laughed away my fear as my partner in joy that evening, Maia, had me change seats with her atop the huge apple peel green Ferris wheel at Parque de la Alameda in Compostela. Earlier that afternoon, when I opened the shutters in my room at the Hotel Compostela, I could see this, Spain's tallest Ferris wheel, perched high above the cityscape.

My thrill-seeking inner child could not wait to celebrate getting the certificate proving I had achieved my goal of walking over a hundred miles on the Camino by taking a ride on this city attraction.

One of the silly games I played with myself during the landmark journey was to neatly fill up my Credencial with specialty stamps. These ink marks were proof of walking and could be obtained at hotels, churches, monasteries, and cafes. By contrast, the joy stamp of overcoming my fear of being stranded, swinging over the red clay-tiled rooftops of the town below, was not marked anywhere but in my heart. As I eased into the experience and looked out over the Cathedral, and out toward hillsides far off into the distance, I felt the pride of accomplishment.

The Ferris wheel brought back fond memories as it spun around its axis to the blaring sounds of 1970's music like "I Will Survive" (Gloria Gaynor) and "Stayin' Alive" (the Bee Gees). My terror turned to laughter, then awe, when my riding partner broke into the chicken dance. Throughout the journey, Maia had embodied the powerful archetype of the Fool to me. She was a carefree and unpredictable spirit who moving with spontaneity to her own rhythm. Her real name, often associated with fertility and childbirth in Hawaiian culture, fit her perfectly. She played a crucial role during my walk, constantly bringing forward new ideas, trying new foods, and exploring experiences with the wonder of a childlike mind. As you might expect, she was a Cabino.

I eventually loosened my white-knuckle grip on the green iron safety bar as I flashed back to the one-and-done, 10,000-foot tandem jump I had made from a crop-dusting plane years before. One of the few things I remember about that experience was the sign next to the sliding plug door that read "Humpty Dumpty was pushed." The "shove" from the plane came from the skilled skydiver who was harnessed to me and in control of the jump. My fear, which was captured on film, immediately turned to laughter. As soon as I was flying through the blue sky, I began laughing like a hyena.

Back then, I had to rely upon the experienced skydiver. On the Ferris wheel I had to rely upon the experienced wheel operator and my friend, who showed no fear as we dangled 200 feet above the earth. Eventually, my fear turned to laughter and some ease, and like the unforgettable thrill of jumping, I tasted awe once again.

There is something special about seeing nature from a bird's-eye view. Until I jumped, the idea of a God-shaped hand with lakes was only a concept.

Looking back at this ride once safely on the earth, I was reminded that the tandem jump marked the end of a cycle in my life. Back then, it was seventeen years of living and growing into my adult self in Syracuse, New York. I am certain the Ferris wheel in Galicia was like putting the dot on the "i" of my Camino. I was left to wonder if awe is always on the flipside of the fear coin.

The group laughed at every lunch and dinner. One woman shared the story of rolling around on the ground in laughter. Personally, I am glad I did not walk and laugh simultaneously because an explosion of energy might have used up all my much-needed wind. But I do remember occasional bursts of loud laughter. We laughed while we eased our muscles in the spa pool, with its array of cascading spillways and high-pressured spouts for every area of the body.

Finding the best gelato became a happy sport. My iPhone, on the other hand, became a constant source of amusement. It was always adding unnecessary steps and never once got us to our intended destination without a detour. At the Cathedral, the tour operator finally let me in on the secret—turn off the Wi-Fi to make the GPS work. But it was too late for my pilgrimage by then. We laughed retrospectively at all my wrong turns, including getting lost for the opening dinner. One fellow walker summed it up best: "Ninety-nine out of a hundred times when I took out my phone to figure out where I was, I would miss an arrow or sign. This made me realize how much else I'm missing that's right in front of my face."

It became clear that sometimes it's about putting away the distractions and trusting that the path will reveal itself—if we're paying attention.

The evening before our final walk into Santiago, when a few of us gathered to play poker using a bowl of potpourri as our gambling chips, the sweet-smelling stakes made us laugh and connect. A standing joke between me and my sometimes roomie was "Yoga nidra is better than *Dateline.*" We agreed to replace a habit of watching police drama before bed as white noise with listening to a guided meditation app. This is how life flowed for me while walking the Coastal Camino.

One day, during a particularly long walk from Baiona of over twelve miles, I hit a point where I felt I couldn't take another step forward. The day began peacefully, winding along the Atlantic coast promenade. I walked with Michara Windsong (a Canadian, not her real name), passing popular beaches, ocean grasses, and boardwalks. We stopped at a bustling café in the resort town of Nigran, where locals were enjoying their morning.

As the day progressed, we followed the yellow arrows through old villages, up a windy hillside, and along idyllic forests. We met a nomadic couple who had spent the past two years traveling through South America and Europe, enjoying their retirement years as pilgrims. For a while, we walked with them, sharing stories as we ascended the road. At a roadside café, we paused for bubbly water before continuing our journey, passing a group of cyclists aiding an injured rider.

The road led us back to a long stretch of beach, past bathers and even a nude beach—no pictures were taken. Then, out of nowhere, I burst into song: *"I've been working on the railroad, all the live-long day . . . ,"* Michara joined in. And together, we sang, *"Fee fi fiddley aye-oh, strumming the old banjo!"* The music lifted our spirits, giving us the energy to keep going and setting a rhythm for our steps.

We repeated this part of the song for blocks, until we at last reached the hotel. It made that last quarter of a mile doable, and we entered the hotel feeling strong, happy, and laughing. Through song and laughter, we were connected.

"Enlighten up" is my motto. Each class I teach begins with a group laughter session because joy raises the vibration of ourselves and those around us. You can feel joy when you walk into a space where people recently were laughing.

During the final leg of my journey, I wanted to be in Santiago for the Pilgrim's Mass. I got up extra early and was sneaking out of the hotel before the Power Walkers could get a firm lead on me when, in my haste, I tripped going through the doorway and skinned my knee. I laughed at my sixty-six-year-old competitive self, got up, dusted myself off, and slowly headed out.

Leaving at daybreak to conquer the final nine miles was my own private joke. My reasoning was twofold: First, I wanted to arrive early at the Cathedral to get a seat for the mass, and second, after two weeks of tying my Hoka sneakers every morning ready to race forward, I knew I could not keep pace with the walkers who were a third of my age. They always left right after the 8:30 AM breakfast.

This would be a shorter walk than most. It began in the small town of Teo, Spain, where pilgrims are led down a maze of stone walls that overlooks wide patches of green. Like most of the other inland walking days, there were the blue and yellow signs showing the way down city streets, weaving you in and out of civilization and forests.

I loved completing the journey solo.

The night before, I had circled up the pilgrims for a closing ceremony that included a wind-clearing exercise. We had an amazing dinner event at the Parada de Francos Restaurant, which was connected to the country hotel where some of us would sleep.

The walk to Teo had been bittersweet. It was drizzling that day, our only day that hinted of impending rain. The journey had passed its tipping point, and I felt the end near, closing in around me. Whereas at the end of the first day's walk, I wondered how my decrepit feet with their bunions and spurs would ever take me to the finish line, now I felt a nostalgic longing.

As we left Padron, the melancholy increased. Although there was more laughter and fun at the start of the day, the group was ultimately split in two. Several of us had stayed the night before at an inn called Os Lambráns. As writers, many of us felt right at home in Padron, so I was not surprised to learn that this town was the home of two important writers: poet Rosalía de Castro and Camilo José Cela, winner of the 1989 Nobel Prize for Literature.

At a stone marker that read "Km 6,339" in La Coruña, Spain, I noticed the carved yellow arrow pointing towards Compostela, and I began to sing again. (In Spain, commas are used as decimal separators the way Americans use decimal points. For us, this would've read 6.339, which is an illogical distance to commemorate however you do.) At that moment, I didn't realize the numbers weren't accurate distance markers. However, I estimated I had about four miles left to walk.

KM 40.800

This time, I sang Girl Scout camp songs I had not thought about in years. These were not the later songs I sang when I was a camp counselor during college, but the primary ones from when I was seven and first went away to overnight camp. I knew it was my years of survival training while camping in the woods that extended throughout my life to make these last three or four miles joyful. I sang out loud as I walked through the quiet towns in the early morning light and through the final forest before entering the busy streets of Santiago de Compostela.

That day's walk felt like a celebration of Spirit and was emblematic of what I would willingly sacrifice for more joy in my life.

The pain came and went through the entire trip, but singing always put love in my heart, a smile on my face, and a skip in my step.

Reflection Questions

What brings you joy, and how can you incorporate more of it into your life?

When was the last time you laughed so hard that it hurt?

How could you create moments of joy and laughter, even in challenging times?

What song or activity lifts your spirits when you're feeling down?

How do you balance moments of lightness with deeper reflection in your daily life?

....

Let Go

*"I suppose in the end, the whole of life
becomes an act of letting go, but what always
hurts the most is not taking a moment to
say goodbye."*

DAVID MAGEE

A year of letting go was upon me—letting go of
ideas about retirement, losing friends, and
redefining home. I felt like I was drifting in a boat on
a turbulent sea. On my first full day in Portugal, I
walked along the beach in Porto, where the sound of
waves crashing against the shoreline reminded me
that letting go was inevitable but didn't need to be
frightening. In the harbor, boats bobbed up and
down, both tethered and free. As I watched the
ocean release each wave, I felt both safely anchored
and protected, much like those boats. As the sea

pulled back, I imagined myself releasing my old ideas of home, career, and the purpose of this pilgrimage. I felt part of the ebb and flow of that late afternoon and of my own life. Life, much like a pilgrimage, contains cycles of release.

Throughout the year of my Camino, I felt those cycles strongly—letting go of not only physical possessions but also identities and relationships. The first week along the coast reminded me that nothing is permanent. As I followed the trail along the sea, the waves crashing against the volcanic rocks showed me that just as the ocean releases its grip on the shore, so too must we release our hold on the things we cannot control—whether it be loss, aging, our group of pilgrims, or the illusions of immortality. Whether it's letting go of a career or grieving for those we've lost, every goodbye shapes us, and it's this realization that pushes us forward.

Soul searching often begins when we feel triggered, stuck, or spinning in an endless cycle of disappointment. Soul searching often begins with an inability to let go. Many years ago, despite my achievements as a hotel chef, I found myself in the HR office at the Hyatt, facing a final written warning. My inability to get along with my coworkers had reached a breaking point. I lacked respect for them, feeling particularly entitled and bitter since that first day in the kitchen was filled with the smell of scorched tomatoes. Cooking had chosen me in my twenties, providing the right-hand turn I needed to overcome addiction and depression. My career as a chef was once a salvation. But eventually, it became clear that I had outgrown it. My time as a chef, filled with successes and challenges, culminated in a pivotal moment of letting go. Letting go of that role felt like losing a part of myself, but it opened a door to new opportunities and deeper spiritual work.

To respectfully know ourselves as active reflections of the divine requires us to make a surefooted walk between responsibility for ourselves and for the community, and I was wobbling. But because I was hardworking and had marketing talents, it was my good fortune that the Director of Food and Beverage plucked me from the kitchen and put me into front-of-house management, giving me a reprieve from the unemployment line and a way to pivot in career direction, without me completely letting go.

Not everyone feels trapped by a mundane career. But from my earliest memories of riding the train to New York City from the town where I lived, I was on a quest for something greater. I craved magic and purpose. Tears filled my eyes on the first day I went to work at General Electric after college, already realizing that the job I'd been hired to do would not align with my soul.

Beside my youthful arrogance, I was irresponsible. After repeatedly missing many days of work and not returning from lunch, my employers grew tired of my lack of commitment and charm, and I was let go. Although getting dismissed for poor performance felt like a cowardly way to let go of a path that didn't serve me, I was glad of it.

After being let go from my job, I felt both lost and relieved, as if the universe had nudged me off a path that was never truly mine. But the uncertainty of where to go next weighed heavily on me. It was during this time that I turned to a psychiatrist, Dr. Short, for guidance. Following a battery of tests and a dozen or so sessions, Dr. Short gave me a practical road map for introspection. He acknowledged my quest for meaning, suggesting that for many women such quests often commence much later in life.

Some of Dr. Short's insights about my condition stung, though in retrospect I can see that they were my initial catalyst for spiritual growth. One of the things I appreciated that he did was to teach me how my mind works—how I can get attached to a paralyzing or painful idea. In many ways, he helped me understand the process of letting go.

Standing in the HR office at General Electric, facing the consequences of my choices, it wasn't just about losing a job—it was about shedding an identity. My inexperience in business made me believe I needed to cling to this corporate path, even though I felt deep down that it wasn't right for me.

My reluctance to leave the job at GE would be mirrored at intervals throughout my life by my reluctance to take a stand for myself. Walking the Camino step by step brought me face to face with similar resistance. Letting go of the identity I thought I was supposed to be—whether that of a driven chef or a capable pilgrim—was as hard as leaving behind that early corporate career. Both times, I found myself asking: *Who am I, if not this?*

And that's the core of it—letting go of an identity can feel like a threat to our very survival. We cling to the roles and labels we've given ourselves because they make us feel safe, even when they no longer serve us. Whether it was my corporate job or the miles I believed I had to walk, it was attachment that held me back. Only by releasing my attachments—

by surrendering to the uncertainty of who I was becoming—could I make space for something new.

Chronic depression is like being stranded in a tiny boat on the ocean with a Bengal tiger like Pi was in *Life of Pi*. In that story, Pi's survival is dependent on letting go of what he cannot control. In my own life, I had to let go of both my control over external circumstances and an internal struggle with depression. Just as Pi respected the tiger, I had to respect the forces within me. My journey to sobriety and creative freedom was shaped by this act of letting go—an essential surrender to the tides of life.

Dr. Short motivated me to explore deeper aspects of myself, ultimately leading me to quit drinking and pursue a spiritual solution to my life. Much like Pi's journey, I came to realize that survival and growth depend on acknowledging and respecting the forces that shape us—whether it's depression or inner conflict—guiding us toward a life more aligned with our spirit.

As I walked solo from Arcade to Pontevedra, I passed through ornate cemeteries, where ancient stone mausoleums embossed with saints stood silent, their columns crowned with crosses, quietly watching over generations past. I paused, reflecting on the many people I had lost that year. In those moments of solitude, I couldn't help but think about the sacrifices made by the Knights Templar. Their story reminds us that sometimes the most profound sacrifices we make are more than purely physical; they're spiritual as well. Like them, I was learning to release my attachment to worldly roles, titles, and identities that no longer served me.

Just as the Templars shed their titles to live in service to a higher calling, I, too, was shedding the title of professional chef and driven seeker—labels I had carried for too long. The Camino was my initiation into the art of letting go, much like the Templars who faced surrender with grace.

On one *lápida* (tombstone), a cat rested in the morning sun, immediately reminding me of Dash, a long-gone, much-beloved calico companion who had helped me through some of the darkest periods of depression and self-exploration. This cat, resting among these stones, seemed a gentle reminder that transitions—whether of lives, titles, or even identities—are natural, even necessary. I paused, realizing how often the living need the dead to remind us of our own transformations.

The uneven stones along the path were slowing other pilgrims as well; I noticed their slower pace, even with the aid of walking poles. Just when my feet were aching beyond tolerance, a small cathedral appeared on the horizon, offering a place to rest. Despite the bustling inside, I found a quiet corner to light a candle, honoring all my feline friends who had come and gone throughout my life.

Our daily responsibility as pilgrims in the pursuit of divine truth lies in our ability to risk, talk to other pilgrims, let go, and surrender to happiness. The first two tenets of the twelve-step program of Alcoholics Anonymous, which could be viewed as a sobriety pilgrimage, are about powerlessness and surrender. Powerlessness is the respectful cry for help, and surrender is the sacred wisdom revealed once we let go and step onto the path of sober living.

In my life, I have realized that while my happiness depends on nothing—no *thing*—awakening occurs when I can locate the sacred ground of the divine and surrender to it. The paradox of surrendering to the divine is that we will never be successful without the support of the divine. Some call this support *grace*. I have found wisdom in the journey of letting go and letting God do its work on my mortal being, which is what makes me a pilgrim.

Ultimately, letting go is a profound act of respect—respect for yourself and for the cycles that guide your life. Whether it was my career as a chef or the friends and roles I've left behind, the act of letting go became my map. Each cycle of release shaped me. And as I learned, it's only by letting go that we create space for growth and new beginnings.

Demonstrating respect for others requires me to accept people as my equals, no matter what choices they make. The other chefs in the Hyatt kitchen who burned the tomato sauce and took shortcuts in their cooking were my equals, but I didn't treat them as such.

On the Camino, I practiced showing respect to my walking companions by not taking things personally—or when I did, by consciously letting go and transforming resentment into something more constructive. For instance, one day I wanted to share a ride with the SAS subgroup and walk together. The plan for the day was to skip an industrial stretch of the Camino about sixteen miles long that lay in an urban region between Vigo and Redondela by taking cabs to our next starting point in Arcade. When I was told that the SAS cab was full, I initially felt excluded. But instead of letting that feeling fester, I let it go by discussing it in my 11:11 AM post.

Feeling left out has been a recurring theme in my life, so letting go felt like an act of respect toward myself, the sacred land, and the other pilgrims who walked before me. Letting go of hurt feelings was an important lesson for the day, but like the steep hill we crossed just days earlier after Vila Praia de Âncora, letting go of old expectations—especially the assumption that others understood my needs—was exhausting but necessary. I remembered how, after reaching the top of a particular hill, I was rewarded with a newfound sense of lightness, clarity, and a beautiful view, knowing that my journey was mine to walk, even if it meant walking alone sometimes. On this day, it became clear that I needed to express my desires more openly, even if it meant risking disappointment.

The experience of feeling left out helped me learn the lesson of speaking up for my needs. My fellow group members served as valuable mirrors for me. I gained awareness and insights from my interactions with them that reflected to me both my strengths and areas where I needed to develop.

Just as understanding the physical terrain of the Camino helps a pilgrim handle the challenges of walking, recognizing our emotional starting points helps us handle our inner challenges, such as setting goals, letting go of old habits, and progressing toward a healthy, balanced state of being.

In my life, as I have grown spiritually, I've learned to embrace the idea that everything is alive with Spirit, including endings and letting go of how we feel about certain outcomes.

Reflection Questions

Are there titles or roles you have held on to that are no longer serving your highest purpose? How might you begin to release them?

Is there something you're holding on to that no longer serves your growth?

How can you practice self-compassion when you let go of something meaningful?

What part of your physical journey mirrors your emotional process of letting go?

How could you practice more intentionality in your spiritual journey?

What fears arise when you consider letting go, and how can you face them?

....

Follow Your Heart

"But the beauty is in the walking—we are
betrayed by destinations."

GWYN THOMAS

The search for meaning is a common theme throughout the centuries in myth, storytelling, and religion. In Insight Two, I shared a story about the hero's journey from King Arthur. It is written that the Holy Grail was found by Sir Galahad, the son of Sir Lancelot, who was depicted as the purest and most virtuous of King Arthur's knights. His success in finding the Grail in this story symbolizes spiritual purity and divine favor.

The quest for the Holy Grail is one of the most famous elements of Arthurian legend, representing the knights' pursuit of spiritual perfection and the divine mysteries. Similarly, the search for the Holy

Grail could be at the heart of each pilgrim who hears the call and undertakes the personal journey.

What is in your heart? How do you serve? Your body, as your vessel of service, carries your soul and spirit. While your spirit may be everlasting, your body gets only one chance at life. Make it count.

I am grateful that I undertook my pilgrimage with a naive purity because, through it, I recovered something I had not known I had even lost. Joy.

Even months after completing the Camino, both my physical recovery and the spiritual insights continued to unfold. In August, months following the walk, I was reminded of Don, the shaman friend who'd reconnected with me after more than a decade. I recalled how, when he heard about my upcoming pilgrimage, he'd gifted me with *Walking Home* by Sonia Choquette and asked me to carry his spirit with me on the journey. I had assumed his inability to walk stemmed from physical limitations, so I gratefully sent him videos and messages from the trail, feeling I was offering support from afar.

Months after returning home, a sharp spiritual "knock at the door" came at 4 AM, waking me with an intuitive message: "Check in with Don, he is gone." When such messages arrive, they do so with urgency, and this one was no different. I learned that Don had passed away shortly after I left Porto to begin my walk. His request to be part of my journey had been a silent cry for connection in his final days, and I had missed it.

The realization that someone I hadn't seen in over a decade had made such a profound impact on my year—and my journey—is a reminder that waiting is a luxury we often don't have. Don's spirit had guided me through the Camino in ways I hadn't fully realized until it was too late to tell him.

The lesson is that we must follow our hearts *now,* reach out, call, and be present for the people who matter *now.* The time to act is *now,* not later.

Don was a significant and guiding force in my spiritual awakening, and I had only fully recognized it when the opportunity to connect was gone.

A once avid daily walker in the wind, today I feel walked out, much like the time I gave up my utensils when burned out from too much cooking. Hiking presently seems to me like a snow-covered peak beyond reach. Unlike my thirty-year-old self, who prematurely sold all her catering equipment, I am patient and taking shorter walks to build up my stamina again.

On a recent short walk, I learned to forage for chanterelle mushrooms near my home. I began envisioning taking more pilgrims on walkabouts.

Advanced training may have helped me avoid putting severe wear and tear strain on my physical body—or maybe not. As someone on a fast-moving "train" through life, the time of not walking and slowing down to write that produced this book has been a significant piece of my Camino experience.

A literary search for books about the Camino, led me to the discovery that countless people who walked before me integrated their ideas into well-documented pages and chapters. The solitude of writing has safeguarded my experience from being picked apart by questions from non-walkers. Were these other walker-writers as protective of their experience when asked "What was it like?" with honest curiosity?

My answer to this query is always the same: "You might need to go and walk this or walk another path to find out why a quest for your truth is tugging at your heart."

Before I began my Camino adventure, I wondered if I would have a supernatural or mystical experience along the way. While I did not have specific expectations of connecting with earlier lifetimes, I was curious if I would feel a connection to the Knights Templar, like both Shirley MacLaine and Sonia Choquette before me did. They felt the Templars' spiritual protection, guidance, and inner strength during their pilgrimages. The Knights Templar, often seen as guardians of sacred knowledge and spiritual warriors, align with the journey of self-discovery and spiritual awakening that many seek on such a path.

The Knights Templar, a medieval Christian military order founded in 1119 CE, were not only protectors of pilgrims but also emblematic of deep sacrifice and service to a higher cause. Through facing the perils of their mission, they came to symbolize the internal courage and strength necessary for undertaking any transformative journey.

The Templars ultimately faced a tragic fate when King Philip IV of France, driven by greed and political motivation, ordered their arrest on false charges of heresy in 1307. The execution of the order's grand master, Jacques de Molay, in 1314 marked the end of the Templars' physical presence, but their legacy endures.

The Templars' unwavering devotion to their cause is reminiscent of the sacrifices we each, too, must make when we commit to personal growth and inner transformation.

As we walk our own paths, we may not face literal trials like the Templars, but the inner battles—of letting go of old beliefs, facing fears, or releasing attachments—require of us just as much bravery.

Are you willing to make sacrifices for your growth? Where do you stand firm in your journey, even when you're faced with inner doubt?

While I did not transcend time or feel an other-worldly connection during my Camino, I did say prayers along the way for all the pilgrims throughout history that had walked the trails before me, and for all the ones who would follow going forward in time, and for people like my mom, whose window for walking one hundred-plus miles has closed.

I hope this book filled your pilgrim spirit with insight and wonder, too. I walked for you.

While researching the Knights Templar, I initially misinterpreted their origination date as being 1118 CE, and got excited because the numerals in that date add up to eleven. Although most historians report the year as 1119, I am still struck by how much of a theme the sequence of 111 has been for my journey and this book. In some interpretations, particularly within numerology, the integers of 1118 adding up to 11 (1 + 1 + 1 + 8 = 11) is seen as significant because the number eleven is associated with spiritual awakening, enlightenment, and insight. Eleven is sometimes referred to as a Master Number in numerology and is thought to carry a high level of spiritual vibration.

This mystical interpretation is not generally emphasized in historical accounts of the Knights Templar. Still it was significant for my journey. Walking the Camino served as a powerful reminder to me of the importance of listening to my inner guidance, making decisions from my heart, and lovingly integrating the lessons learned on the path into my everyday life.

Throughout the eleven days of walking, ritual and ceremony played a significant role in my pilgrimage. Before walking every morning and during group gatherings, I would perform a wind whistling ceremony for myself or the group. *Wind whistling* is a way of making a prayer to the spirits of air, calling on them for guidance and support—a practice I explain in detail in my book *Winds of*

Spirit. Paying attention to wind messengers was key to how I received guidance throughout the Camino.

In many religious traditions, including the Christian tradition whose theology permeates the Camino, the Holy Spirit is described as the biblical breath of wind, invisible and arriving seemingly from nowhere. This philosophy informed how I moved along the trail, stopping to listen and changing course as the wind guided me. It was an honor to invite other walkers to share this ancient tradition.

It was also clear that water rituals would be an important element of my walking experience, especially as I walked along the Portuguese Coastal Route of the Camino. Before I even stepped foot on the trail, I took a riverboat and visited Praia do Carneiro, a beach next to a sixteenth-century fort in Porto. On the very first walking day, I left the charming seaside village of Viana do Castelo, moving at a steady pace along real cobblestones and rutted stone pavers while breathing in the views of the expansive Atlantic Ocean.

Spain and Portugal are renowned for their tin-glazed, blue ceramic tiles known as *azulejo.* After losing my way and finding myself on a winding path, I stumbled upon my first pilgrim fountain, or *fuente,* made from azulejo. Nestled deep in the woods, this ancient stone fountain felt like a sacred discovery. These fountains, often found in villages, monasteries, or along the roadside, have long provided fresh water to pilgrims walking the Camino. Many are centuries old, integral to the pilgrimage's history, and adorned with inscriptions, religious symbols, or artwork reflecting the spiritual journey to Santiago de Compostela. In quiet reverence, I rinsed my hands and face, symbolically cleansing my expectations. As I prepared for the 120 miles ahead, I invited the Knights Templar to watch over me, opening myself to the wisdom and insights that would unfold as I walked in a state of devotion.

After leaving that place, I walked down the hill to the boardwalk at the beach, a guaranteed route to Vila Praia de Ancora. On day one, I was still naive about pacing myself to accomplish the full day's walk ahead of me. I leisurely stopped, took off my shoes and socks, and felt the cold ocean on my legs. Following my dip, I met with three other walkers from our trip, who were assembling founders of the SAS subgroup. It was a long, slow walk for me, and I quickly learned that going that slowly wasn't a pace I would cherish for long. Still, I was grateful to spend the afternoon learning about the SAS team and their impetus for joining the Wind and Stars walkabout.

The first was from Romania, the second from the United Kingdom, and the third from Oregon. Ours was quite an international group.

Throughout the pilgrimage, water held a profound significance, and I felt a deep sense of loss when we finally moved inland after seven days of walking along the coast. However, the path still offered solace through a series of fast-moving streams, rivers, and waterfalls we encountered. On the seventh day of walking, the trail led across the Verdugo River. Red-tiled rooftops dotted the hillside here, illuminated by the soft glow of the early morning sun as I recorded and posted my morning reflection on Instagram at 11:11 AM local time.

Crossing the narrow Ponte Sampaio, a bridge shared by both pilgrims and cars, I marveled at its architecture, unaware at the time of its historical importance during the 1809 Battle of Ponte Sampaio, a key moment in the Napoleonic Wars.

That day, I walked solo for the entire eleven miles. The trail began with a steep ascent into the hillside, and my feet, already worn down by the uneven stone paths, protested with each step. Yet the morning was lightened with moments of joy, starting with the unexpected sight of a bagpiper playing along the trail. Water became a constant metaphor, its presence washing away my tendency to take myself too seriously. When I stumbled upon a noisy beer garden in the woods, I felt irritation bubbling up, but I reminded myself to embrace nonjudgment for others and self-compassion. These disruptions, much like the streams and rivers I crossed, reminded me to flow with the noise and challenges of the walk, rather than resist them.

That afternoon, just a few miles before reaching a large scallop monument welcoming pilgrims to Pontevedra, I had the chance to embrace the shift in my experience. The day had started with a steep climb along the highway, but by the afternoon, the trail descended into a shaded, steady path that wound around a stream. Finding a quiet spot to remove my shoes and reflect in silence wasn't possible, so I pressed forward, letting the rubber of my worn soles carry me through. Instead, I spent time chatting with fellow pilgrims while soaking my feet, particularly enjoying the company of a couple from Barcelona, who were walking for the weekend. We met again at the finish line at the Cathedral of Santiago de Compostela, sharing a moment of mutual accomplishment.

There is an ongoing process of healing, and I am learning the value of being patient with myself as I continue to unravel the Camino experience. One immediate shift is my unwillingness to spend my entire life working without time for play. Recently, friends were in town, and I took a day off midweek to enjoy a late summer outing. I've made it clear to my employers that I bring wisdom, not just the brawn of "doing." I've set boundaries at work, particularly when it comes to working longer hours.

I suspect these changes will continue to inform my experience as we move into the new year and beyond. All my life, I've valued myself as a doer, and tied my worth to the calluses on my hands. Now, I want to move into a phase where I mentor others to handle the heavier lifting. This pilgrimage showed me that I have often used work as an excuse for my inability to be available and present for those I love. Life is too short to regret the time we have left with those we cherish.

There was another moment, days before arriving in Compostela, when the miles before me seemed like an insurmountable path through a eucalyptus forest with no sun in sight. The walk between A Guarda and Baiona was long and I was walking like I was on a mission to go nonstop from point A to point B. In retrospect, I regret not stopping at the sweet cafe perched on a hillside for fresh-squeezed orange juice. I was being impatient as the proprietor took his time treating each customer like they were the only one in line. *Sweet man.*

I used the outhouse, then headed down the beautiful Camino path through the lush country-side. When I hobbled into the hotel, I found my room in the attic. Although the ceilings were low, there was an arched window framing the beach below that in my exhaustion looked like it was too many steps away from me to take a swim.

Literally it was out the back door, but I counted the walking days ahead, and thought, *No way.* Luckily, I had scheduled a massage for that evening, which shifted everything. As the sun rose the next morning, I moved forward with humility and acceptance of everyone on our trip.

I walked each subsequent day knowing that it was with grace that I was able to put one foot before the next, one walking pole supporting me as I went.

As I walked into Santiago de Compostela, I found myself singing *Dona nobis pacem*, a beautiful three-part round, humming and singing each part for the final mile. The Latin hymn, which means "Grant us peace," felt like a perfect companion for this last stretch of my journey. As the path turned into the city, I met a fellow pilgrim from my home state of Washington. Like me, she was approaching the end of her pilgrimage to receive the *Compostela,* a certificate given at the completion of the Camino, to those who visit the Tomb of Saint James. She shared that she had walked with minimal belongings and camped outside whenever possible, holding a vision of peace on Earth as she walked.

We kept each other company through the busy city blocks, but as her pace quickened, I found myself struggling to keep up. I decided to pause, letting her walk ahead up the hill toward the Cathedral of Santiago de Compostela. I stopped for my final cappuccino, savoring the moment, as I realized the journey was nearing its end. Memories of the past ten days—and of all the other journeys in my life that had led me there—flooded my mind.

In my heart, I knew my pilgrimage wasn't just about reaching the cathedral or completing the trek. While the excitement grew as the cathedral spire loomed into view, this walk had always been about something more profound.

The heart's true calling lies in the act of moving forward—one step at a time, one release at a time— whether through valleys of doubt or hills of insight.

Each step was a testament to letting go, to following my inner compass no matter the obstacles.

I arrived at Obradoiro Square outside the cathedral at 10:37 AM. Seeing that the numbers on my watch added up to eleven was a moment of synchronicity I couldn't ignore. Pilgrims from around the world filled the square, speaking in many languages, each seeking their moment to stand before the grand façade and capture a photo in front

of the iconic cathedral. Luckily, our tour operator, Victoria, spotted me from her place on the waist-high stone wall and snapped a few photos, filled with orbs of light—little reminders of divine guidance. She then directed me toward the Pilgrim's Reception Office, reminding me to hurry over as the line to get a certificate would only grow longer the closer we got to the impending noon mass.

At the Pilgrim's Reception Office, the ritual of receiving the Compostela began with the filling out of my information—my country, the purpose of my pilgrimage, and the route I had walked. To be eligible, a pilgrim's journey must have been undertaken with a heart seeking spiritual or religious meaning, or at the very least, with a spirit of inquiry. The stamps on my Credencial del Peregrino provided my proof of walking the required minimum of one hundred kilometers (sixty-two miles). After an interview in which I was asked to verify my journey, I was handed the long-anticipated certificate.

Holding this document in my hands, I realized the pilgrimage wasn't just about the physical distance I had walked; it was about the emotional and spiritual miles I had traveled, the inner journey of release, and the layers of fear, habits, and self that I had let go of along the way.

As I left the Pilgrim's Reception Office, I saw that the line behind me now stretched out the door. That day, 2,116 pilgrims would arrive to claim a

Compostela, each with their own story to tell about their own journey. I wondered about their reasons for walking. *Were they seeking release, like me?*

When I entered the cathedral, the pews were already full, but I found a spot at the base of a massive stone column where I could lean my back. From there, I had a clear view of the altar and the Botafumeiro, the grand incense burner that occasionally swings during the Pilgrim's Mass. Nearby me, I noticed a couple I had met creek side a few days before. They stood hand in hand, their faces glowing with a quiet joy that seemed to radiate throughout the room. Their connection was palpable—an exuberance that softened the solemnity of the cathedral, making the air feel lighter, more alive. We exchanged warm smiles, a silent acknowledgment of our shared journey.

Although the mass was conducted in Spanish, a language I barely understood, the sacredness of the space transcended language barriers. I felt the collective heartbeat of the pilgrims around me, each of us connected to the millions who had walked this path before, our stories woven together by each step we'd taken. The cathedral, with its towering columns and hallowed stones, whispered the stories of earlier pilgrims, reminding me that while my journey was uniquely mine, it was also part of something far greater—a timeless pilgrimage shared by countless souls seeking peace, truth, and renewal.

While the Botafumeiro remained still that day, its presence was palpable. I envisioned it carrying the prayers of centuries of pilgrims into the sacred air, a bridge between the earthly and the divine. This journey, while deeply personal, connected us all to something eternal—a pilgrimage shared across time and space by millions of people walking toward their own revelations. Hundreds of thousands every year.

After about forty-five minutes of mass, certain that the great thurible would not swing, I wandered to the cathedral shop and purchased a special blend of incense—Compostela Blend—for a personal ceremony in the future. Though the smoke didn't fill the space that day, the brass, bronze, and silver censer remained a spectacle, hanging from its sixty-five-foot rope under the great dome of the cathedral. Historically, it was used to cleanse the air of the scent of pilgrims, who often arrived after weeks of walking without proper washing. Its symbolic meaning, though, transcends its practical use; it is a visual and olfactory reminder of the sacredness of the journey and the prayers carried forth into the ether.

As I stepped out of the cathedral and into the square to meet some fellow pilgrims for lunch, I knew my journey was far from over. Physically, I had reached the end, but my heart whispered that there were more paths to follow, more steps to take. I realized then that following my heart isn't a one time act; it is a continuous unfolding, a lifelong journey of listening, trusting, and moving forward with courage and grace. My pilgrimage was not a conclusion, but the opening of a new chapter.

While receiving the Compostela may mark the end of the physical Camino, I know that the lessons, the self-discovery, and the transformation I experienced on that journey will guide me on countless inner pilgrimages yet to come. The heart's true calling doesn't end at a particular destination—it's in the continuous unfolding of each step forward, each moment of surrender, and each time we dare to follow its pull.

Reflection Questions

What does the idea of "following your heart" mean to you, and how can you trust your heart's guidance when the path ahead seems unclear or uncertain?

Reflecting on sacrifices and inner courage, where in your life are you being called to let go of old beliefs or attachments in order to grow?

Do you feel called to take a spiritual pilgrimage, whether physical or metaphorical? How might you be more attentive in listening to that call?

Consider a time when you've arrived at a personal or emotional crossroads. How did you make that transition, and what lessons did you carry forward?

How can you embrace the idea that your own journey can never truly be complete, but will be a continuous unfolding of growth and discovery?

EPILOGUE

How can you continue to walk your soul's path, following the wisdom and guidance of your heart, even when the road ahead is unclear?

As you close this book, I invite you to reflect on your own Way (*Camino*), whatever form it may take. Life itself is a pilgrimage, filled with unexpected twists, challenges, and moments of deep reflection. As one member of our group shared months after the trip, "Maybe it wasn't the trip itself that upended my life, maybe it was always there in my destiny and the time just coincided." While the path looks different for each of us, the journey toward the heart is universal. Whether you choose to walk the Camino de Santiago, answer a calling, or take small, daily steps, I hope that you find clarity, healing, and a renewed sense of purpose.

As I look back on the journey, I realize that the yellow arrows and clamshell markers don't just guide pilgrims along the Camino—they are signposts guiding us on an internal journey. Each one is a reminder to stop, notice, and trust the insights we receive, even when we aren't sure where the path will lead. The path doesn't generally reveal itself all at once to a pilgrim, but the markers are always there, quietly pointing the way.

May you find the markers on your own path—whether they be arrows, moments of clarity, or quiet whispers of the heart—guiding you home.

For me, the journey of the Camino involved the internal exploration of my judgments. During my walk, Spirit gifted me the following deepening practice, and I hope it encourages you to discover your own tools from what nature freely provides.

Returning the Stones of Judgment: A Deepening Practice

This practice is designed to help you become more aware of your judgments and cultivate greater tolerance for others and acceptance of yourself. It's a simple, tangible activity you can easily integrate into any kind of daily routine.

Step 1. Gather your materials. Find a small bag or pouch that you can carry with you throughout the day.

Step 2. Set your intention. Begin by setting an intention to be mindful of your judgments. You might ask, "Where in my life am I judgmental and intolerant?"

Step 3. Notice your judgments. Look for clues in nature as you walk, at work, or at home, noticing your internal judgments of people, things, and events—even of yourself. Each time you recognize a judgment, pick up a small stone and place it in your bag. Let the stone symbolize the new awareness.

Step 4. Reflect on the stones at the end of the day. Find a quiet place to sit undisturbed. Take out your bag, count the stones, and reflect on the types of judgments you made. Consider how these ideas affected your mood and interactions.

Step 5. Forgive yourself. Hold the stones in your hands and take a few deep breaths. Say the affirmation below as many times as necessary for its full meaning to sink in:

"I forgive myself for my judgments. I release them and embrace compassion."

As you speak these words and let go of each judgment, imagine the weight of the stones lifting from your hands.

Step 6. Return the stones to the earth. If possible, wash the stones under running water. Then, return the cleansed stones to the earth.

By doing this deepening practice regularly, you'll cultivate a deeper sense of nonjudgmental tolerance and acceptance in your daily life.

It's unnecessary to walk the trails of the Camino de Santiago to experience the richness of a pilgrimage. Sometimes getting the deepening we need is as simple as taking a wind walk in nature, where every step becomes a meditation, a practice in listening to your heart.

You might carry one small stone in your pocket, as I did on the Camino, setting the intention to release an old burden or belief at some point on your journey. When you are ready to let it go—whether at the foot of a tree or beside a river, or at the deli where you get your morning coffee—know that by leaving the stone behind you are intentionally making space for something new to emerge.

ACKNOWLEDGMENTS

To the women of the Wind and Stars Walkabout on the Camino: Thank you for sharing not only your time and stories, but also your sore feet. Especially to Loki (you know who you are), our time came, and it was legendary. Who knew taxis and tapas could coexist with a pilgrimage?

To my friends and family, who love me even when I disappear down rabbit holes of whimsy, whether grand or small: Thank you for supporting me through every twist, turn, and epiphany. You're the best traveling companions on this crazy ride, and yes, I know I owe you all dinner.

To my brilliant editor, Stephanie Gunning, who somehow taught me to write despite my attempts to derail the process. Her genius is matched only by her ability to tolerate my last-minute changes. Thank you for pushing me to the finish line. Your guidance is the wind beneath these words.

Lastly, to the winds that keep whispering. May we always listen.

END NOTES

Insight 1: Make a Sacrifice

Epigraph. *The Poetic Edda,* translated by Carolyne Larrington (Oxford: Oxford University Press, 1996): p. 34. The Hávamál is a poem in Old Norse from the *Codex Regius,* originating in the Viking era.

Insight 2: Say Yes to the Call

Epigraph. Rainer Maria Rilke. *Letters to a Young Poet,* translated by M. D. Herter Norton (New York: W.W. Norton & Company, 1934).

Insight 3: Preparation Is Key

Epigraph. Tristan Gooley. *The Lost Art of Reading Nature's Signs: Use Outdoor Clues to Find Your Way, Predict the Weather, Locate Water, Track Animals—and Other Forgotten Skills* (New York: The Experiment, 2015): p. 9.

1. Roland Monsegu. "Who Is Saint James," CaminoWays.com (October 4, 2023).

Insight 4: Take One Step at a Time

Epigraph. Mary Oliver (1935–2019) was a Pulitzer Prize- and National Book Award-winning American poet whose works explored the intersection between humans and the natural world.

Insight 5: Ask a Better Question

Epigraph. Jacqueline Novogratz. *Manifesto for a Moral Revolution: Practices to Build a Better World* (New York: Henry Holt and Company, 2020).

Insight 6: Embrace Nonjudgmental Tolerance and Acceptance

Epigraph. Paulo Coelho. *The Alchemist: 25th Anniversary Edition*, translated by Alan R. Clarke (New York: HarperOne, 2014): p. 155. Originally published in Portuguese in 1988.

Insight 7: Drop the Should-Haves, Could-Haves, and Would-Haves

Epigraph. Mark Twain (1835–1910) was a writer, humorist, and essayist. Source unknown.

Insight 8: Rest Is Essential

Epigraph. Ovid (43 BCE–17 CE) was an ancient Roman poet. Source unknown.

1. The Los Coyotes Reservation is located approximately seventy miles from San Diego, between the Cleveland National Forest and the Anza-Borrego Desert State Park. Members of the band are descendants of the Cahuilla and Cupeña tribes.

Insight 9: Sing a Song

Epigraph. Joan Walsh Anglund. *A Cup of Sun* (New York: Harcourt Brace Jovanovich, 1967): p 15.

Insight 10: Let Go

David Magee. *Life of Pi* (film script), 20th Century Fox, 2012. Based on the original novel by Yann Martel (Orlando, FL.: Harcourt Books, 2001).

Insight 11: Follow Your Heart

Epigraph. Gwyn Thomas (1936–2016), National Poet of Wales. Source unknown.

COPYRIGHT CREDITS

Grateful acknowledgement is made for permission to reprint an excerpt from "The Journey" from *Dream Work* by Mary Oliver in the following territories. Any third-party use of this material, outside of this publication, is prohibited.

In the United States, its Territories and Possessions (including Military Bases), and the Republic of the Philippines: Copyright © 1986 by NW Orchard LLC. Used by permission of Penguin Books, an imprint of Penguin Publishing Group, a division of Penguin Random House LLC. All rights reserved.

In Canada: Reprinted by the permission of the Charlotte Sheedy Literary Agency as agent for the author. Copyright © 1986, 2017 by Mary Oliver with permission of Bill Reichblum.

In the United Kingdom, Open Market, and the European Union: Copyright © 1986 by Mary Oliver. Used by permission of Grove/Atlantic, Inc.

RESOURCES

Thank you for reading *A Pilgrim's Guide to Walking Wisdom*. Here are some additional resources that may be of interest to you.

Visit Renee's Website

The PracticalShaman.com

Stay Connected

Facebook: @ThePracticalShaman
Instagram: @ThePracticalShaman
YouTube: @PracticalShaman

Hire Renee to Speak

Renee@thepracticalshaman.com

Podcasts (Available on All Platforms)

The Practical Shaman Podcast

The Shamans Cave Podcast (cohosted with Sandra Ingerman)

Related Products and Services

Wind Whistles and Other Sacred Tools:
ThePracticalShaman.com/store

Evergreen Courses: WindWork.org

Other Books and Products by Renee

Wind Walker's Wisdom Oracle (Enlightenment
Productions, 2024). A deck of sixty-four wind spirit
cards with a companion instructional book.

Special Offer: Use code WWWO to receive
access to The Oracle Circle with purchase.
Enjoy a complimentary one-year
membership at WindWork.org.

*Winds of Spirit: Ancient Wisdom Tools for
Navigating Relationships, Health, and the Divine*
(Hay House, 2018). Winner of the 2018 Nautilus
Award, *Winds of Spirit* is a practical guide to
connecting with powerful wind energies that lead us
toward authentic joy, power, and purpose.

ABOUT THE AUTHOR

RENEE BARIBEAU, the Practical Shaman, is an author, behavioral healthcare executive, inspirational mentor, respected business coach, dynamic spiritual teacher, wind whistler, podcast host, keynote speaker, author of the award-winning Hay House book *Winds of Spirit: Ancient Wisdom Tools for Navigating Relationships, Health, and the Divine* that helps to achieve successful lifestyle practices, and creator of the *Wind Walker's Wisdom Oracle* card deck. She splits her time between residences on Whidbey Island in northern Washington State and Palm Desert, California.

www.ingramcontent.com/pod-product-compliance
Lightning Source LLC
Chambersburg PA
CBHW070700130626
46553CB00005B/1785